50 Interviews: Successful Property Managers

Advice and Winning Strategies from Industry Leaders

VOLUME I (EPISODES 1-25)

by Michael Levy

WISE
MEDIA GROUP

Wise Media Group
Denver, CO

50 Interviews: Successful Property Managers
Copyright © 2010 by Michael Levy
http://PropertyManagers.50interviews.com

ISBN #: 978-0-9822907-7-4
Library of Congress Control Number: 2010921519

Published by
Wise Media Group
444 17th Street, Suite 507
Denver, CO 80202
www.WiseMediaGroup.com

WISE
MEDIA GROUP

First edition.
Printed in the United States of America.

Wise Media Group
Denver, CO

This book is dedicated to my wife, Cathy, and my two lovely daughters, Chelsea and Rebecca. If it were not for their tremendous support and love, this book would not have been possible. I love them all dearly!

ACKNOWLEDGEMENTS

When I started out on this journey to write a book, I had no idea how much effort it would take. There were so many people that contributed, and without their help, this book would never have been completed.

So, I would like to sincerely thank the following people:

The 25 property managers who agreed to give their valuable time to do the interviews with me and to offer their help in anyway I needed: Susan Albern, Michael Daniels, Tony A. Drost, Dennis Fassett, Bonnie Golden, Glenn Gonzales, Dave Holt, Paul Kaplan, Mark Kreditor, Bill Levy, Dori Locke, Tracey Logan, Mark Mascia, Mia Melle, Matt Middel, Beverly Perina, Diana Pittro, Melissa Prandi, Jennifer S. Ruelens, Raymond Scarabosio, Jessica Scully, Mitch Stephen, Kyle Stephenson, Tom Stokes, and Mark Walters.

The other writers and contributors that provided the very valuable content for the three appendices listed at the end of this book: Paul Farrer, Nat Kunes, and Ginny Sawyer. Thank you also, to Aimee Miller, VP of Marketing at AppFolio, Inc. in Goleta, California, who provided significant assistance and encouragement for this book.

Bob and Lucille Steiner for their encouragement, support, and feedback on some of the initial book cover designs.

My family, friends, and colleagues who have given me so much support, inspiration, and encouragement throughout the entire process of publishing this book. And also my business partners in my three businesses: Prue Kaley, my partner with NorthernColoradoRentals.com, LLC, Mike Robichaud, my partner with NoCoAds, and Cathy Hettleman, my partner with Levy Consulting, LLC.

My fellow board members of the Northern Colorado Rental Housing Association (NoCoRHA) who have provided me with a tremendous education on the property management industry: Robert Miller, Anna Barbre, Melissa Emerson, Dick Eshelman, Kris Farnsworth, Paul Farrer, Carrie Gillis, Belinda Kernaghan, Jeannie Ortega, Beverly Perina, Stephanie Schilling, Sandy Shoen, and Robert Valois.

The numerous transcribers, editors, and layout specialists that helped pulled all the pieces together for this book: Betsy Osgood, Veronica Yager, Tiffany Garofalo, Erin Stettler, Devin Soper, and Nick Zelinger.

My very supportive mother, Harriet Levy, as well as my father, Donald Levy, who taught me much of what I now know about property management. Through his help and coaching, I have been able to effectively manage a number of my own rental properties (residential and vacation) for the last 25+ years. My two brothers, David Levy and Rick Levy. David, a partner with Levy, Erlanger & Company, CPAs in San Francisco, California, founded his company in 1986 for the purpose of providing high-quality financial services to California community associations. Rick is the Chief Financial Officer with SCOLR Pharma, Inc. in Bothell, Washington.

And last, but certainly not least, a million thank you's to Brian Schwartz, the founder and publisher of the 50 Interviews brand. Brian has been an incredible person to work with. His support, inspiration, and tireless enthusiasm have been invaluable to me throughout the entire process.

There are countless more individuals, that although I may not have mentioned them here, I am ever grateful to each and every one of them for their contributions to the creation of this book.

TABLE OF CONTENTS

INTRODUCTION

In late 2009, I embarked on this journey to write a book about successful property managers. My goal was to pull together valuable advice, tips, and winning strategies from some of the most successful property managers in the country. The targeted reader audience is both individuals considering property management as a career option, as well as veteran property managers interested in learning from other successful property managers in the industry.

This book, Volume I, is a collection of interviews with 25 residential property managers from across the United States. Although there are many commonalities among the interviewees, there are also a vast array of unique approaches that are described throughout the interviews.

One common theme was the importance of networking and belonging to some of the most successful organizations in the property management industry, specifically the National Association of Residential Property Managers (NARPM) and the National Apartment Association (NAA) were mentioned more than any others. The importance of good communication and people interaction skills were also mentioned quite often. With respect to the biggest challenges being faced by property managers, the economy was a clear stand out. What was most interesting, is how everyone looked at the challenges from a different perspective and dealt with the issues in different ways. I was also fascinated by the diversity of answers to the question related to what they looked for in their employees.

I had a great time doing the interviews and editing them into this Volume I edition.

Volume II will be a collection of interviews with another 25 property managers specializing in commercial, vacation, association, and residential property management.

It is not possible to include the complete content of all the interviews in this book, so I have started a blog for those interested in reading more about these successful property managers. You may visit the blog at propertymanagers.50interviews.com. I will also include many other additional resources for property managers including discussion forums, tips and advice for property managers as well as individual landlords, property management news, and much more.

"I look for employees with a positive attitude and a good work ethic."
Susan Albern, Rocky Mountain Property Management

◆

BACKGROUND

Susan Albern lives in Loveland, Colorado. Susan began working for Rocky Mountain Property Management in 1995, and with her husband bought the business from Dave Stickler in 1999. Their company is now organized around a homeowner's association (HOA) division, a maintenance division, and a rental division. They currently manage 612 rental units consisting of single-family homes, duplexes, triplexes, fourplexes, and small apartment buildings. They also manage 28 HOAs, comprising over 3,000 units.

INTERVIEW

Q: How did you get into property management?

A: I met Dave Stickler while we were both volunteering at Youth Empire (later Boys and Girls Club of Larimer County). He saw that I had a certain capability, and offered me a job as a property manager.

Q: Did you have a mentor at the time?

A: Just about everybody turns out to be a mentor in one way or another! Dave Stickler was certainly one of them; David Tilney, members and leaders of the National Association of Residential Property Managers (NARPM) like Melissa Prandi, Dave Holt, Steve Urie, Bob Machado, Mark Kreditor, Tony Drost, Betty Fletcher, and Ray Scarabosio, just to name a few. NARPM itself is phenomenal and I've been active on the national front of this organization, meeting hundreds of people who have been wonderful mentors. You share the same problems and don't feel like you're always re-inventing the wheel.

Q: What educational classes have you taken that have proven to be particularly valuable to you?

A: All of the NARPM designation classes have been helpful because they're specifically geared towards property management.

Q: How do you keep up on all the laws that are affecting your property management business?

A: I keep up by watching TV and talking with colleagues, but primarily by being a member of lots of listservs, like those offered by the state and NARPM.

Q: Any recommended books, websites, or other educational resources that you would recommend?

A: I just research the Internet with keywords until I find something really useful. I also tend to be a big listener of audio books, especially when driving to and from work every day. Some of my favorites are Steven Covey's *Seven Habits of Highly Effective People*, Michael Gerber's *E-Myth*, and *What Got You Here Won't Get You There* by Marshall Goldman.

Q: Are you a member of any other professional organizations?

A: I belong to the Community Associations Institute (CAI).

Q: How have you used the Internet in your property management business?

A: It's actually changed the face of doing business. You can solicit or find local and national businesses, research potential tenants, get the word out on your company and keep an eye on the competition. There are even grading and evaluation sites, but you have to keep in mind that they're mostly opinion, and monitor that.

Q: Do you use Craigslist?

A: I don't like Craigslist, but it gets us leads. We've had many problems with it: pirated ads, mudslinging at our company, the parameters change all the time. I don't know a manager out there who likes it, but I use it because that's where people are looking these days.

Q: Do you still do anything with traditional advertising?

A: There are people who still don't have Internet access, so they will pick up a newspaper or look in the Yellow Pages. A lot of my colleagues have given up completely on both, but I still advertise there.

Q: What do you attribute your success to?

A: I've been successful because of hard work, being visionary and able to break things down into steps, and there's a whole lot of luck in there too. Participating in trade organizations is becoming more and more critical; the trend of the future is partnerships. Everybody gets stronger that way. It's not about being competitors, it's about being colleagues and calling on each other when we need help.

> **PROPERTY MANAGERS SHOULD PARTICIPATE IN TRADE ORGANIZATIONS LIKE NARPM – UNDERSTANDING THAT IT'S NOT ABOUT BEING COMPETITORS, IT'S ABOUT BEING COLLEAGUES. EVERYBODY GETS STRONGER THROUGH PARTNERSHIPS.**

SUSAN ALBERN

Q: Where do you draw your strength or inspiration from when things get particularly bleak?

A: I try to get away to rejuvenate by going to the mountains or scuba diving, where you just give your brain a break from it all. But then I don't get Internet there and find myself going through withdrawals.

Q: Are there any particular slogans that you use either personally or in your office?

A: "Do or do not. There is no try," by Yoda.

Q: How do you attract and retain the best employees?

A: We match people's skills, interests, and abilities with tasks that need to be done. I'm definitely blessed with my staff and the skill sets that we have. We take care of our employees and do everything that we can to make their lives better.

Q: What's the most important attribute you look for in an employee?

A: We want a positive attitude and a good work ethic. You can teach skills but you can't teach somebody to care, and you can't teach somebody with a negative outlook on life to be positive.

> **"Do or do not. There is no try." - Yoda**

Q: What are you doing now in your property management business that you feel you should have been doing sooner?

A: Learning to delegate was hard for me.

Q: What are the biggest mistakes you see new property managers making?

A: New managers too often don't take advantage of professional networks. They spend all this energy creating what other people have already done.

Q: What are some of the biggest challenges that you face?

A: One challenge is the societal shift in attitudes that I'm seeing. People take less responsibility for behaviors and say, "It's not my fault" —"I violated the lease because my girlfriend left me with two dogs." Another is the recent economic changes, although fortunately our state has been somewhat insulated from the worst of them. There may still be a ripple effect from places like Phoenix, Las Vegas, Florida and California.

Q: Any tips or tricks that have really helped you in some way to avoid repeating the same mistake?

A: I made a pact with myself a long time ago to never make the same mistake twice. If something doesn't go the way it was supposed to, I always ask myself the cause: "What worked, what didn't, what do we need to do better?" It's almost never the people involved; nobody blatantly sets out to screw something up. It's usually a process or system that didn't go far enough, like the training that someone needed.

Q: Describe your best client and your best tenant.

A: My best client simply understands that rentals are a business. A lot of investors are in the rental market now only because they weren't able to sell their property. But the best client understands that you have to maintain the property in order to keep it going, and not just milk

> **MY FAVORITE TENANT PAYS THE RENT ON TIME, TAKES GOOD CARE OF THE PLACE, AND DOES NOT VIOLATE THE LEASE.**

then bulldoze it. We like being appreciated for the work that we do, of course. All a tenant has to do to be my best tenant is pay the rent on time, take good care of the place, respect the property and the lease.

Q: What have been the most rewarding aspects of your property management business?

A: I love that this job is so diverse. I never come to work and do the same thing twice; I don't usually even hear the same excuse twice! I take a lot of pride and comfort in doing a good job for people. I like the challenge and reward of providing a valuable service in an industry that's difficult and complex.

Q: What do you see as some of the biggest opportunities for new property managers?

A: Property managers are at the hub of a lot of activity and opportunity. If a tenant wants to buy a house, or an owner

SUSAN ALBERN

wants to sell, a property manager can facilitate the sale. A property manager can maintain properties for owners very well with repairs and upgrades. By cultivating their many relationships with insurance brokers, mortgage brokers, and other contacts, managers can facilitate all kinds of mutually beneficial situations.

ROCKY MOUNTAIN PROPERTY MANAGEMENT

2

"Communication and organization skills are the most important attributes we look for in employees."

Michael Daniels, Cagan Management Group

◆

BACKGROUND

Michael Daniels lives in Lincolnwood, Illinois. He has been in the property management field for over 25 years. Michael is one of the principals of the Cagan Management Group (CMG) and the Director of Property Management for the company. CMG has over 65 employees in Illinois and Florida. Their portfolio of approximately 300 properties consists of 15,000 units in urban apartment buildings, suburban garden style properties, homeowners associations, and a small number of commercial and office buildings.

INTERVIEW

Q: How did you get into property management?

A: I started doing some odd jobs for my high school basketball coach, who was a partner at what was then called Cagan Realty. When I was in my second year of college, majoring in accounting, Jeff Cagan approached me about becoming a property manager. I joined the company almost full time and attended school in the evenings.

Q: When you started to get into property management, did you have a mentor?

A: At that time there were only three other people in the office: Jeff Cagan, his mother Sylvia, and Norman Litz, my former coach. Each one of them handled a different aspect of the business, and together they taught me bookkeeping, accounting, how to put a deal together, and how to handle the day-to-day operations of the properties.

Q: What educational classes have you taken that have been particularly valuable to you?

A: All the Institute of Real Estate Management (IREM) classes are great for educational and networking opportunities. They cover such topics as marketing, management of properties and investments, problem solving, ethics, etc. When we started expanding our homeowners associations and condominium management, we hooked up with the Association of Professional Community Managers (APCM) and took their courses as well. I'm now a Certified Property Manager, a Certified Manager of Community Associations, and an Association Management Specialist.

Q: How do you keep up with the various laws that affect the property management industry?

A: The professional associations of which I'm a member are my best resources for keeping track. They constantly send out newsletters and try to get their members more involved in things that are important to the property management profession.

Q: Are there any books, websites, or other educational resources that you would recommend?

A: I read a lot of management books on how to deal with people, how to be a good boss, and other management-related areas.

Q: What professional organizations do you belong to?

A: The IREM organization is the largest and most recognized organization for general rental property management, and they're also getting a little more involved with homeowners associations now. I'm involved with the APCM, which focuses on condominiums and other types of associations, and I also belong to the National Association of Realtors (NAR).

8

Q: How do you use the Internet in your property management business?

A: A lot of our print media is going by the wayside because most people now use Internet searches like Google to find property managers or apartments. Most of my leads still come from word-of-mouth and the next highest number of leads come from the web. E-mail is a very big part of our day and is one of the primary ways I communicate with my buildings.

Q: Do you use any traditional advertising?

A: The bang for the buck is just no longer there with traditional advertising. We depend on signs a lot because there's still a big trend of people who are looking for apartments to drive, bike, or walk around the neighborhood they're interested in. The number of calls that come in from signage, recommendations from other tenants, and websites including our own, far exceeds the number that we get from any print advertising.

Q: Are you doing any PR to promote your company?

A: In just the last couple of years we've started doing small press releases targeted at local trade and business magazines; for example, when someone is promoted or we take on a new complex. One of our managers was featured in the IREM publication article "30 under 30," which focused on managers under 30 years old who were "on the move." The month after that, I was featured for Cagan being an Accredited Management Organization. We recently signed on with a professional agency to update our image and branding.

Q: What do you attribute your success to?

A: I attribute my success to getting along well with others, just like in kindergarten. I try to demonstrate clear thinking and common sense, and am very straight with people. Being a bit super- organized has helped, too.

Q: When things aren't going too well, where do you draw your

MICHAEL DANIELS

strength or inspiration from?

A: Earlier in my career, if I lost a building or a management account, I would beat myself up over it or try to place blame for it. Now I realize that business is business, and you're going to get along with some people and not others. Somebody else always has a worse problem, so I'm happy to stick with mine.

> **I ATTRIBUTE MY SUCCESS TO GETTING ALONG WELL WITH OTHERS.**

Q: Do you have any particular slogans that you or your company uses?

A: "We manage as if it's our own and we manage to be the best." No one way works for every property or every owner. We don't force people into a mold, and we'll manage with a different style for each property if that's what it takes.

Q: How do you attract and retain the best employees?

A: Empowerment, in a word; I give my people the tools that they need and a lot of room to sink or swim on their own. But I also have an open door policy; I spend a lot of time mentoring managers through situations, and making sure they have enough support staff, equipment, and whatever else they need to succeed. They seem to appreciate that.

Q: What's the most important attribute you look for in an employee?

A: Communication and organization skills are the key to our business, so effective communication is a must – this is where we beat our competition. I often hear complaints from potential new clients about other management companies who don't return calls, or are poorly organized about such things as vendor bids. I use Microsoft Outlook to keep me organized and to communicate as effectively as possible, both inside and outside our company.

Q: What are you doing now in your property management busi-

CAGAN MANAGEMENT GROUP

ness that you wish you had done sooner?

A: I've put more structured processes and standards in place recently, and I wish I had done that earlier on. For example, weekly reports are now given to each owner or client. I'm trying to give them information and updates before they even ask us for them. I now have an operations manager who makes sure the managers get these reports created and sent out on time.

> **THE BIGGEST MISTAKE I SEE NEW PROPERTY MANAGERS MAKING IS WHEN THEY TRY TO "SWEEP PROBLEMS UNDER THE RUG," OR THEY PROCRASTINATE WHEN IT COMES TO ADDRESSING A TOUGH SITUATION.**

Q: What are some of the biggest mistakes you see new property managers make?

A: The biggest mistake I see is when they try to "sweep things under the rug," or they procrastinate when it comes to addressing a tough situation. They think things are going to magically get better or be easier to deal with tomorrow, and they avoid sharing concerns with the client or their supervisor. If new managers deal with problems in a timely manner, typically the client and/or the supervisor will be more understanding.

Q: What are some of the biggest challenges that you face?

A: My biggest challenge is that my clients are now micromanaging me much more than in the past. They do so because occupancy rates are down and so is their cash flow. I get calls from my clients asking why their monthly disbursement checks are, for example, $2,000 versus the $5,000 they had been getting. They're scrutinizing everything, asking many more questions related to expenses and wanting to know the justification for each of those expenses.

MICHAEL DANIELS

Q: How do you overcome those challenges?

A: The best way is to be upfront and provide them with regular reports and updates, to avoid any surprises. We've also started providing clients with some forward-looking forecasts, so they know that disbursements may be delayed while we pay off some of their other investments and expenses.

Q: Describe your best tenant and your best owner.

A: My best owner/client is someone who has managed the property himself or has somehow been involved with the management of it before. It is much easier to deal with him because he understands what can, and does, happen in property management. My best tenant is reasonable, respectful, works with me if there is an issue or a problem, and realizes that things don't always go smoothly. Ninety-five percent of tenants are good ones; it's the other 5% of your tenants who cause 100% of the problems.

> **MY BEST OWNER IS SOMEONE WHO HAS MANAGED THE PROPERTY HIMSELF OR HAS SOMEHOW BEEN INVOLVED WITH THE MANAGEMENT OF IT IN THE PAST.**

Q: What have been the most rewarding aspects of your property management business?

A: One of the most rewarding aspects, for me personally, is that I'm respected by current and past clients and tenants. I feel I could still ask for a reference from people I no longer do business with. We have also won some awards like the "Property Management Company of the Year," which are great to receive. But more important than being recognized in that regard, is not being recognized for anything bad or improper.

Q: What do you see as some of the biggest opportunities for new property managers?

A: For new property managers, one of the biggest opportunities is connecting with companies and banks dealing with troubled assets in these difficult economic times. However, this will require a more educated property manager who is knowledgeable and able to comply with more demanding requirements for reporting and communication. It's all on a higher level and more complex now.

MICHAEL DANIELS

*"Whenever you see a successful business,
someone once made a courageous decision."*
-Peter F. Drucker

3

"The best thing I've learned over the years is the word 'NO'."

Tony Drost, First Rate Property Management

◆

BACKGROUND

Tony Drost has been in property management for over 19 years. He started his own company, First Rate Property Management, in 1994. He now manages over 800 units, including single-family homes, smaller multi-family buildings, and four-plexes (40% of his portfolio). Tony lives in Boise, Idaho.

INTERVIEW

Q: How did you get into property management?

A: In 1990, while still in college, my wife and I moved into our first apartment. It was a disaster. Between theft, neighbors' fights and even fires! We wanted out, so we bought a duplex. A few years later, I sold it at a very nice profit and bought two four-plexes within a 20-building community. My units looked better, had higher rents, and better tenants than the others. So those owners asked me to manage their properties, too. I ended up managing 80 units.

Q: Did you have a mentor?

A: No, I learned from the school of hard knocks. Idaho has no licensing requirements for property managers and very few laws. Eventually I joined the national and local chapters of the National Association of Residential Property Managers (NARPM). Their members look at each other as colleagues, not competitors. I networked with property managers from all over the nation. Before long, I had forms, contracts, policies and procedures, and guidance that made me one of the best. Today, I believe I'm the most educated and experienced property manager in the area.

Q: What educational classes have you taken that have proven to be very valuable to you?

A: I have a BA degree in operations management which gave me the skills to develop and manage a business. However, NARPM taught me the skills to be an effective property manager. I currently hold the Master Property Manager (MPM) and the Residential Property Manager (RPM) designations from NARPM. My employees and I attend all the regional and national NARPM conferences and conventions. These events offer top-notch speakers and workshop instructors, and are very valuable to our business. I receive the *Residential Resource*, an award-winning NARPM magazine which is full of educational articles.

Q: How do you keep up with all the new laws related to property management?

A: Both my local NARPM chapter and NARPM's headquarters keep me informed.

Q: Any recommended books, websites, or other educational resources, that you would recommend?

A: Joining a professional association such as NARPM is essential. Depending on your concentration, single family, apartment buildings, or commercial, I suggest NARPM, IREM, or the Certified Commercial Investment Member (CCIM) Institute. An investor wanting to manage his own properties can look to books on the subject, but I recommend hiring a property manager and letting the expert handle it. Many of the books that I've read were "pie in the sky" schemes: buying with no money down and doing all the

> **IF YOU MANAGE COMMERCIAL OR LARGER MULTI-FAMILY DWELLINGS, YOU SHOULD JOIN THE INSTITUTE OF REAL ESTATE MANAGEMENT (IREM).**

repairs yourself. Most of these properties wind up disasters; it's just not that easy. The Fair Housing Act is a very complicated subject and you can't rely on common sense any more. If you don't have initial and ongoing training on those issues, you could get a hefty fine for an unintentional mistake.

Q: What are you reading now?

A: Reading doesn't fill in the gaps the way class discussions can; taking courses is more beneficial. I've also learned a lot by simply visiting other property managers' offices.

Q: How has the Internet helped you?

A: A good website is very powerful; I had one before the Internet was commonly used. It's now possible to market our properties 24/7/365. E-mail communication with clients and tenants is searchable and retrievable. Owners can go to our site and access statements or balances, transfer funds, read newsletters, and participate in our blog. Tenants can access their accounts, view available properties (with photos and virtual tours), apply or pay their rent online, and read tenant newsletters.

> **IF YOU MANAGE SINGLE FAMILY HOMES AND SMALL MULTI-FAMILY BUILDINGS, YOU SHOULD JOIN THE NATIONAL ASSOCIATION OF RESIDENTIAL PROPERTY MANAGERS (NARPM).**

TONY DROST

Q: Do you use any of the social media tools like Facebook, Twitter, LinkedIn, etc.?

A: I've taken a number of classes on this topic and can certainly see the advantages, but I'll have to find someone with the expertise and time to keep up with it all.

Q: Do you find traditional advertising helpful?

A: Print advertising is so costly. We still do it, but we have cut way back and look forward to stopping it all together.

Q: What about PR/getting in the media (TV, radio, or print)?

A: We evaluate our marketing by calculating a lease/conversion ratio; I'm more interested in leases than in leads. I've done TV and radio ads but, like print advertising, they proved to be far too expensive. Internet advertising generally is lower cost per lease. We've also done bus stop benches and billboards, but our lowest cost per lease advertising is referrals from our tenants and yard signs.

Q: What do you attribute your success to?

A: I am an investor too, so I speak my clients' language. I don't bother them with the small stuff, I communicate the important things and offer good advice so that good decisions can be made quickly.

Q: Where do you draw your strength or inspiration from when things get particularly bleak in your business?

A: When the economy crashes, so does the housing market. With job losses, cut hours, belt-tightening, and the surplus of inventory, our rental market has gotten tough. I can't control the market, so I don't stress about that. I can control how my company handles business, so I focus on that, adapt to the market changes, and think outside the box to come up with new marketing strategies. If my clients are experiencing costly repairs or extended vacancies, I feel their pain and do everything I can to eliminate it. The only thing that gives me strength and inspiration are "thank you's" from our tenants and clients.

> **USING THE INTERNET, OUR OWNERS CAN ACCESS THEIR STATEMENTS, SEE THEIR BALANCE, TRANSFER FUNDS, READ OUR NEWSLETTERS, AND PARTICIPATE IN OUR BLOG.**

Q: How do you attract and retain the best employees?

A: Our best employees come to us as referrals from friends or current employees.

Q: What is the most important attribute you look for?

A: In this business, you are hit with 100 things coming from all directions at once, and you need to keep your cool. Past employees quit or were fired because they were unable to stay organized during chaos. They need to simply take it all in and systematically prioritize everything.

Q: What are you doing now in your property management business that you should have started doing sooner?

A: I wish I'd known about NARPM from the beginning; it would have saved me a lot of time, heartache, and money.

Q: What are some of the biggest challenges you face?

A: Managing property is second nature for me and I pretty much know the answer for just about every situation. However, finding employees who "get it", who work hard, do a great job and make sound decisions, is a challenge. I'm blessed to have several long-time employees who can do this, but teaching property management to new employees has been difficult.

> **USING THE INTERNET, OUR TENANTS CAN ACCESS THEIR ACCOUNTS, VIEW AVAILABLE PROPERTIES, APPLY ONLINE, PAY THEIR RENT ONLINE, AND ALSO READ OUR TENANT NEWSLETTERS.**

TONY DROST

Q: How have you overcome those challenges?

A: It's a constant battle; we change duties, we train, we hire more people to assist. This is definitely my biggest challenge.

Q: Any tips or tricks that have really helped you in some way to avoid repeating the same mistakes?

A: Joining NARPM has been the best thing for me and my company. Honestly, if it weren't for NARPM, I would have gotten burned out years ago and moved on to something different.

Q: Describe your best client.

A: My best client allows my company to manage the property, trusts me, and appreciates my expertise and hard work. Micromanaging by our clients causes mistakes. If we're allowed to do our job, clients are almost always 100% satisfied.

Q: What have been the most rewarding aspects of your property management business?

A: Nothing makes me happier than filling a vacancy faster than expected, with a super tenant who takes great care of it and pays his rent in a timely way. That makes for happy tenants and happy owners.

Q: What do you see as some of the biggest opportunities for new property managers?

A: Focus on your current tenants and clients, and other business will naturally follow. You could lose established customers if you ignore them by focusing too much on getting new clients.

> **THE ONLY THING THAT GIVES ME STRENGTH AND INSPIRATION ARE "THANK YOU'S" FROM OUR TENANTS AND CLIENTS.**

FIRST RATE PROPERTY MANAGEMENT

4

"My keys to success are property selection and tenant screening."

Dennis Fassett, Great Lakes Investment Fund

◆

BACKGROUND

Dennis Fassett lives in Franklin, Michigan. He got started in property management in 2004. He has a full-time, 60 hours per week, corporate finance job and manages his own properties. The properties include 11 single-family homes and a 20-unit apartment building.

INTERVIEW

Q: How did you get into property management?

A: Back in 2004, I decided to create a little safety net for my family. I bought my first rental property in 2005 and have been a property manager ever since. My process starts with management in mind, when I am looking for a property to purchase. I buy the best properties to attract the best tenants, which means going for the best school districts in neighborhoods that people prefer. The houses take two to three hours of attention a week, except when they are turn overs, and they are "set and forget", which is my approach. I have a fantastic occupancy record and a backlog of tenants because people know the quality of my houses. I manage all my properties myself; I love being a landlord. It's been a great experience.

Q: In terms of your "set and forget" policy, it seems like the tenant screening process is probably a big part of that?

A: You hit the nail on the head. The first of two critical steps is the "set it and forget it" property selection. The second is tenant

DENNIS FASSETT

screening, for which I have a rigorous process. I charge the highest security deposits allowed by Michigan law, and cover the background check cost by charging a $35 application fee. The application form requires five years of rental and employment history, and I check all those references (for apartments, three years). I drive by their current residence, and if I have a potential concern, I will even ask to see the inside. It's all geared to doing a little bit of work up front to save myself a lot of work down the road. I am looking for evidence of evictions more than anything else. I also use E-Renter.com.

> **I BUY THE BEST PROPERTIES TO ATTRACT THE BEST TENANTS, AND THAT MEANS GOING FOR THE BEST SCHOOL DISTRICTS IN NEIGHBORHOODS PEOPLE PREFER.**

Q: How do you keep up on the laws that affect property management?

A: In Michigan, the attorney general's office publishes the *Landlord-Tenant Guide*. It's a summary, in plain English, of the laws for rental property owners. I check the state website a couple of times a year and, as a licensed real estate agent, I do continuing education annually for refreshers on rental property law.

Q: Are there any other books, websites, or educational resources that you would recommend?

A: A really good website out there is www.MrLandlord.com. It has some good information, as well as a forum where landlords can get together to talk about various problems and ideas.

Q: How do you use the social media networks to help your business?

A: I put a "For Rent" sign in the window but count on the Internet 100% for filling vacancies, using resources like Rentlinx and Craigslist. Facebook and Twitter help with leads on new properties too. I put myself out there so people know that I am a guy who is looking for "set and forget" houses and apartment buildings in attractive areas to buy, and that I can help train others to do property management the same way I do. My approach has been profiled on CNNMoney.com and in the Wall Street Journal's *SmartMoney* magazine, all because of social media.

Q: Do you have any suggestions or tips for people who are just getting started with using social media tools, to help them with their business?

A: The social media landscape is so broad, people can't possibly use all the different available tools. Focus on Twitter and Facebook, which are now linked so you don't have to update both of them. I've got a Facebook page dedicated to cash flow properties (The Cash Flow Mercenary), and people know they can find me there; I have over 6,000 posts on Twitter. These tools have been a tremendous door-opener for me in terms of networking with other managers and owners, getting ideas, having a window on the global property management realm, and moving forward in my knowledge of the field.

> **FOR ALL RENTAL APPLICANTS, I LOOK AT THEIR LAST FIVE YEARS OF RENTAL HISTORY AND I CALL ALL OF THEIR PREVIOUS LANDLORDS.**

Q: Can you mention some of the tools you use with Twitter?

A: I use TweetDeck; it's a free tool for grouping and managing other people's Twitter updates. I have a multi-family group set up in there so that whenever conversation happens about management for apartment buildings, I can follow it and preserve it. Twellow is a directory of people who use Twitter.

Q: What do you attribute your success to?

A: I've spent the last four years streamlining and using a sys-

DENNIS FASSETT

tematic, standardized approach. I have checklists and procedures for everything so I don't even have to think about it. I realized that a robust and thorough tenant screening process would give me great tenants. Focus and persistence are key.

Q: Is there anything that you are doing now in property management that you wish you had done sooner or learned sooner?

A: I wish I had my approach in place from the beginning, which probably would have helped my first ventures. I should have done referral bonuses earlier; I've found that the best prospective renter can be a friend or acquaintance of one of my current tenants.

Q: What are the biggest mistakes you see new property managers making?

A: Never let tenants get control. I see new managers letting tenants negotiate away things that are set down in their lease agreements, like when their rent is due. They don't send eviction notices the day after rent is late. I have a very strict set of guidelines. I set expectations up front, and I stand by them, but I also temper that with flexibility when legitimate issues come up. New property managers should be very diligent and maintain control of the landlord/tenant relationship.

> **WITH MY TENANTS, I HAVE A VERY STRICT SET OF GUIDELINES. I SET EXPECTATIONS UP FRONT, AND I STAND BY THEM, BUT I ALSO TEMPER THAT WITH FLEXIBILITY WHEN LEGITIMATE ISSUES COME UP.**

Q: What are some of the biggest challenges that you face?

A: People are leaving the Detroit metro area, and apartment buildings like mine, are feeling a bit of that pinch. When that happens, the challenge is that it takes more time to find tenants for the apartments, and there's some downward pressure on the rental rates.

Q: Describe your best client and your best tenant.

A: I never hear from my best tenants! They take great care of the house and landscaping, plant flowers every year, and they pay their rent and utilities on time every month.

Q: What has been the most rewarding aspect of your property management business?

A: Property management has provided an income for my family, but it has also helped me to really develop my people skills. I've met wonderful people, including some of my tenants.

Q: What do you see as some of the biggest opportunities for new property managers?

A: The biggest opportunity right now is all the social media tools on the Internet, and I encourage managers to fully use them. When I open the newspaper and see a bunch of rental property ads, I just shake my head.

> **THE BIGGEST OPPORTUNITY RIGHT NOW FOR PROPERTY MANAGERS IS TO LEVERAGE SOME OF THE SOCIAL MEDIA TOOLS ON THE INTERNET.**

DENNIS FASSETT

*"Whatever made you successful in the past,
won't in the future."*

-Lew Platt

5

"Keep at it. Just keep at it. Don't give up."
**Bonnie Golden, Golden Rentals &
Management Services, LLC**

◆

BACKGROUND

Bonnie Golden lives in Taos, New Mexico. Bonnie sold her original property management company after five years, in 2007, and started another property management company, Golden Rentals & Management Services, in 2009. She has been in the industry for 13 years and currently manages approximately 100 vacation and residential properties.

Bonnie's key to being a successful property manager:
"I believe success comes from treating tenants with dignity and respect, being certain their living conditions are safe and healthy, responding quickly to repairs, as well as following Fair Housing laws and state regulations. A big part of the business requires that you manage your owners, too. It is very important to develop a good relationship with your owners so they understand that you're not trying to nickel and dime them when you tell them a new washing machine is needed, but rather that you are merely taking care of their property. Having a good reputation for well-maintained properties drives business to you as a property manager. Referral business with professionals and other business members within the community helps, too."

INTERVIEW

Q: How did you get into property management?

A: I received my real estate license in the beginning of 2002. I went to work for Coldwell Banker and after a couple of weeks, I realized that I did not want to do real estate and that I preferred property management. I managed a nursing home and that is where I got my feet wet learning what goes on with a large physical plant. Next, I managed a hotel which included management of the physical property. After I talked with the owner/broker of Coldwell Banker Lota Realty, we decided to open a property management division and that launched my new career.

Q: How did you learn about being a property manager?

A: If you are very organized and have some sort of business savvy, you can do it. Most states require that you are licensed either through the real estate commission or through some organization within the state. I immediately joined the National Association of Residential Property Managers (NARPM) and Vacation Rental Managers Association (VRMA). From both of those groups, I learned about business ethics, management of properties, dealing with owners and tenants, and the various laws as they pertain to property management. Any professional, in any profession, owes it to their clients to belong to an association so they can continue to learn and grow as rules and regulations evolve in their industry.

> **WE POST SOME OF OUR VACATION PROPERTIES ON VRBO.COM AND HOMEAWAY.COM. THEY ARE DEFINITELY GOOD WEBSITES.**

Q: How have you leveraged the Internet for your business?

A: You absolutely have to have a website, especially if you are doing vacation rentals, because you need to reach out to the people who are looking for a place to stay. You want to be at the top of that search page, whether they go to Google or another search engine. I immediately started out with a website. We also post some of our vacation properties on VRBO.com and HomeAway.com as long as the owner agrees to pay for that service. These are definitely good websites. But the newspaper, *The Taos News*, is our best resource in finding long-term tenants.

Q: Do you do any PR for your company?

A: Yes, whenever anything noteworthy happens, I send out a press release. Living in a relatively small town, I have been able to get my name out to the local community frequently via press releases. I have been interviewed on the radio and there was a nice, long article, about me two summers ago in one of the newspaper supplements. I think you have to work all of your angles.

> **WHENEVER ANYTHING NOTEWORTHY HAPPENS, I SEND OUT A PRESS RELEASE. YOU HAVE TO WORK ALL OF YOUR ANGLES.**

Q: What do you attribute your success to?

A: Integrity, honesty, and treating people fairly and openly. A lot of people are disrespectful to tenants and you can't be. They are your customers. They are out in the community and they are the people who will talk about you. I treat my employees really well and that has also been a key to my success.

Q: Where do you draw your strength and inspiration from when things get particularly bleak in your business?

A: I draw strength from my co-workers. We can discuss issues, discuss what's going on, and pull one another up if somebody is having a difficult time.

Q: Any slogans you or your company use?

A: "Keep at it. Just keep at it. Don't give up."

Q: How do you attract and retain the best employees?

A: A lot of hiring here is by word of mouth but I also put ads in the paper. I pay better than most companies. I pay new hires on an hourly basis and then after a three to six month probation period, they go on salary. I offer health benefits, a gym club membership, basically something that is of value to that

BONNIE GOLDEN

person as opposed to saying, "This is the way it is for everybody." For instance, one woman requested a flexible schedule because she had an infant, so we set that up for her.

Q: What is the most important attribute you look for?

A: A sense of humor. Also, in property management, an important attribute is the ability to multi-task. Everybody does everything. So multi-tasking is supreme. In my opinion, if somebody is a linear thinker, they cannot do property management.

Q: What are you doing now in your property management business you should have started doing sooner?

A: I should have been more discriminating in the properties that I took on in the beginning because there were quite a few that were sub-par and that had extremely difficult owners. It was hard to extricate myself from them.

Q: What are the biggest mistakes you see new property managers making?

A: Spending too much time with problem owners. It's not only an energy drain, but it's a financial drain. Problem owners just don't want to spend the money and they fight you on everything. I see no reason to deal with them. You need to interview the owners just like you would an employee and a tenant. Explain your expectations and your policies.

Q: What are some of the biggest challenges you face?

A: I think the biggest challenge right now is the economy. Historically, when the real estate market is bad, the rental market is good. But since it's not just the real estate market that is bad right now, it's everything, we are having to lower rental rates, whether it's a vacation rental or a long-term rental, and that's difficult. A lot of owners aren't making their mortgage payments off of their monthly rental income, so they are frustrated too. Everybody is hurting, so it's a challenge all the way around.

Golden Rentals & Management Services, LLC

Q: Describe your best client/owner.

A: I think the best client is somebody who is a clear communicator, has reasonable objectives for the property, and is not argumentative.

Q: What have been the most rewarding aspects of your property management business?

A: Watching it grow and the ability to pay bonuses and increase employee benefits. It makes me feel good to see money coming in through hard work and long hours and being able to write a check to an employee who has helped me reach my goals. Property management is also very exhausting, downright exhausting! Especially around the holidays from mid-December to New Years. It's really hard working seven days a week, ten to twelve hours a day. Sometimes you are called out and have to meet the plumber or the handyman at two o'clock in the morning if your regular guy isn't available. So, it's tiring, but it's also rewarding too! It's fun. It's never boring. Ever.

> **THE BEST CLIENT (E.G. LANDLORD/OWNER) IS SOMEBODY WHO IS A CLEAR COMMUNICATOR, HAS REASONABLE OBJECTIVES FOR THE PROPERTY, AND IS NOT ARGUMENTATIVE.**

BONNIE GOLDEN

Q: What do you see as some of the biggest opportunities for new property managers?

A: In this market, I think that there is a lot of opportunity with foreclosures and working with banks. I think there's a huge opportunity out there, if you want to hustle and make some money.

"Never tell people how to do things. Tell them what to do and they will surprise you with their ingenuity."

-George S. Patton

6

"Put the right people in the right place doing the right things."

Glenn Gonzales, PPA Real Estate Management

◆

BACKGROUND

Glenn Gonzales lives in Austin, Texas. He has over 20 years of experience in property management. Glenn is currently the president of PPA Real Estate Management, established in 2008. The company has 65 employees and manages a total of 11 multi-family properties located in Dallas, Waco, and San Antonio, Texas.

INTERVIEW

Q: How did you get into property management?

A: While I was going to college, I got a job doing some maintenance work for a property management company. That position led me to steady growth from part-time manager for a 60-unit apartment complex, to regional manager, to Director of Operations. I took additional training specifically in the multi-family industry, got my real estate license, and earned the Certified Property Management (CPM) designation from the Institute of Real Estate Management (IREM).

Q: When you got started in property management, did you have a mentor?

A: Dale Longhurst was the president of the company and my first mentor. He inspired me to get more specific education in the property management field. Later on, John Gibson became my mentor, and an inspiration. He was a self-made millionaire who bought apartment complexes and renovated them from scratch. He taught me that I could do the same

GLENN GONZALES

thing if I really wanted to, and showed me how. I eventually bought an apartment complex from him and had some success with that.

Q: Any educational classes that you've taken that have proven particularly valuable to you?

A: There are several offered by the apartment association, like the Certified Apartment Manager (CAM) course. IREM offers a Certified Property Management (CPM) designation. Those are great classes covering management, human resources, budgeting, marketing, financing of apartments, and returns on investments.

Q: How do you keep track of all of the laws that affect your property management business?

A: I stay very involved with the local associations, and I serve on the governmental affairs committee. I'm also a member of the National Apartment Association (NAA).

Q: Are there any recommended books, websites or other educational resources you would recommend?

A: The websites for NAA and IREM are very good resources. Some excellent books I've read are *FYI: For Your Improvement, A Guide for Development and Coaching* by Michael Lombardo, *Give 'em the Pickle!* by Robert Farrell, and *Who Moved My Cheese?* by Spencer Johnson, MD.

Q: Do you use the Internet, and if so, how has it helped your company?

A: We use several statistical-based websites like Reis.com. They give us information on rental rates, rental growth, absorption rates, new construction permits, and available units that are coming online or that are being taken offline due to condo conversions. This kind of information is key to your occupancy rates and the amount of rent you charge; it gets right back to basic supply and demand principles. It helps me with executive decisions on my budgeting, rent growth, and possible rent declines. For day-to-day operations and to check up on my competition, I use ForRent.com, ApartmentGuide.com, and Apartments.com.

Q: What do you attribute your success to?

A: I find mentors, people who absolutely love the business, and ask them all kinds of questions. Successful people love to share stories with you about how they achieved their goals. Everybody's got their different ways of doing things, but they all seem to have persistence and determination in common.

Q: When things aren't going so well, where do you draw your strength and inspiration from?

A: Mostly from within myself; I often tell myself if this job were easy, everybody would do it. If someone tells me "It can't be done," I take that more as a challenge than a roadblock. I'll call one of my mentors and ask if he's ever come across a certain situation before. He'll usually send me away feeling good about myself, and that's typically of more benefit than actually being told how to fix the problem.

> **WEBSITES LIKE REIS.COM ARE STATISTICAL-BASED WEBSITES THAT GIVE US GREAT INFORMATION ON RENTAL RATES, RENTAL GROWTH, ABSORPTION RATES, NEW CONSTRUCTION PERMITS, ETC.**

Q: Are there any other slogans that either you or your company use?

A: "Put the right people in the right place doing the right things." That has proven to be a great formula for me when it comes to managing employees.

Q: How do you attract and retain the best employees?

A: I spend a great deal of time personally mentoring and teaching my managers. I recently gave all of them a great book called *Zapp! The Lightning of Empowerment: How to Improve*

GLENN GONZALES

Productivity, Quality, and Employee Satisfaction by William Byham and Jeff Cox. I don't have much turnover, because I empower them to be leaders, not just managers.

Q: What's the most important attribute that you look for in an employee?

A: I look for honesty. I interviewed two people this week and I ended up hiring the person with less experience. On her resume, she was completely honest and said she wasn't familiar with a particular software program that we use in our company. The other candidate said that she did have experience with the software, but when I tested her on it, she clearly wasn't being totally honest about her experience.

Q: What are you doing now in property management that you wish you had done sooner?

A: My personality is such that I want to try to make everybody happy. I probably would have had less turnover and fewer headaches overall, if I had learned a lot sooner in my career that you can't do it all, and that sometimes you have to say "no." I'd have learned earlier to "put the right people in the right place" as well.

Q: What are some of the biggest mistakes you see new property managers making?

A: Managers today are getting complacent because in the past they've managed properties in a very healthy environment with high occupancy rates and rents. They need to re-think their skill sets in terms of tenant issues, public relations, negotiations, and marketing. People have choices today, competition is tough, so tenant retention is more important than it has ever been.

> **THE MOST IMPORTANT ATTRIBUTE FOR AN EMPLOYEE TO HAVE IS HONESTY.**

Q: What are some of the biggest challenges that you face?

A: Rents are getting lower, concessions are going up, and occupancies are going down. All of those variables at the end of the day cause me to have less income, but my expenses have not gone down. My challenge is continually trying to find creative ways to cut costs without giving up on the customer service end.

Q: Describe your best tenant.

A: I love the tenant who reaches out and provides me feedback that I can then use to improve our customer service. My tenants can call me all day long even if they have a complaint; because if one resident feels that way, I guarantee you others do, too.

Q: What's the most rewarding aspect of your property management business?

A: I love a good challenge, to take an underperforming property that nobody else could fix, and turn it around. I have the attitude that if nobody else can fix it, I can, with the right people in the right places, doing the right things. I'll do everything I can to make sure our customers are taken care of, and we beat our competition. I've bought some communities, personally increased their value and then sold them for a profit, which was very rewarding. Just to hear somebody say "thank you" goes a long way with me, too.

> **I LOVE THE TENANT WHO REACHES OUT AND PROVIDES ME FEEDBACK THAT I CAN THEN USE TO IMPROVE OUR CUSTOMER SERVICE.**

Q: What are some of the biggest opportunities you see for new property managers?

A: Somebody coming into our business today can really get educated and have a lot of fun doing it! My advice is to learn everything you can and make it a career.

GLENN GONZALES

"To improve is to change. To be perfect is to change often."

-Winston Churchill

7

"Whatever you can conceive and believe, you can achieve."
Dave Holt, Residential Property Management, Inc.

◆

BACKGROUND

Dave Holt lives in Minneapolis, Minnesota. Dave has 25 years of experience in property management and is the president of Residential Property Management, established in 1989. His company has 10 employees and oversees almost 400 residential properties, 90% of which are single-family houses.

INTERVIEW

Q: How did you get into property management?

A: Just out of college I started a business called Home Sitters. We would arrange for people to stay in vacant homes, in exchange for a small rent fee. Eventually we started managing foreclosed properties for the U. S. Department of Housing and Urban Development. In 1989, we began doing fee-management for others and that's when Residential Property Management was started.

Q: Are there any educational classes that you have taken, that you have found to be particularly valuable?

A: The National Association of Residential Property Managers (NARPM) has designation courses and workshops on a wide range of topics that focus on single-family property management. There are also many valuable classes from The Institute of Real Estate Management's (IREM) Certified Property Manager (CPM) program.

Q: How do you keep up with all the laws that affect your property management business?

A: You have to be proactive in getting such information, and stay involved with professional organizations. I subscribe to several periodicals, and I check websites for national and state legislation changes.

Q: Are there any specific periodicals or websites you would recommend?

A: Some good periodicals are *Landlord Tenant Bulletin, Fair Housing Coach, Professional Property Manager* (from the Apartment Association), and *The Advocate* (from our local multi-housing group). Some good websites are RentLaw.com and RentalProp.com. I also suggest your state attorney general's office for such resources as tenant/landlord handbooks, which summarize a lot of the important statutes landlords should know about.

Q: Are there any other books or other educational resources you would recommend?

A: The books I have found most beneficial involve organizing and systematizing all the things you have to handle on a daily basis. Property management has so many different tasks and laws associated with it, and you have to do things consistently. One very valuable book is *On Getting Things Done* by David Allen. Another is Michael Gerber's *E-Myth*. It really helps you look at your business from a different point of view and create the systems that are necessary to make it work for you. I've really taken that concept to heart and I think it is key in any business, but especially property management. An older but timeless book is Napoleon Hill's *Think and Grow Rich*, which really gets you to focus on your major purpose.

> **Some good websites are RentLaw.com and RentalProp.com.**

Q: How do you use the Internet for your property management business and how has it helped you?

A: The Internet has provided us a tool to improve our organization. It's made us more efficient and more consistent, which is especially important when it comes to property management law.

Q: Do you still do anything in the traditional advertising space?
A: We really don't use much traditional advertising any more. It's expensive compared to the Internet, and media such as the Yellow Pages and the newspapers are going online anyway.

Q: Are you using Craigslist and is that working for you?
A: Yes, we use Craigslist as well as other sites; however, Craigslist has become one of the largest sources of fraud out there. Scammers take your information, pose as landlords, break into properties, re-key and "rent" them to unsuspecting tenants and take their money. It's really too bad, and I don't know what the solution is for something like that.

> **WE CAN ALL LEARN FROM WHAT OTHER SUCCESSFUL PEOPLE DO.**

Q: Do you do anything else for PR for your company, such as TV or radio?
A: It's certainly not as effective, and very costly. Not many companies buy TV or radio ads now, especially in the single-family home market. On the other hand, if you receive positive PR for free through an article in the newspaper or an interview on the radio, that is definitely a good thing to take advantage of.

Q: What do you attribute your success to?
A: We can all learn from what other successful people do; it saves so much time and effort. For example, Napoleon Hill put that concept into his book of interviews with the elite business people of his time. I also use a lot of what Edward

DAVE HOLT

Deming taught about his concept of constant and never-ending improvement.

Q: Where do you draw your strength and inspiration from when things don't go particularly well for you?

A: I learned about self-affirmations from Napoleon Hill, "Whatever you can conceive and believe, you can achieve." I recite an affirmation every day that gets me focused on my purpose and all the positive things that I have in my life. If you respond to challenges in a defensive and stressful manner, they'll take a toll on you. But if you welcome and learn from them as part of the growth process, everything's a lot easier to deal with.

Q: Are there any slogans that you personally live by or that you use within your company?

A: "Whatever you can conceive and believe, you can achieve." That's from Napoleon Hill and I recite it every day. I do live by that and also Deming's constant and never-ending improvement, which is part of our company's mission.

Q: How do you attract and retain the best employees?

A: Property management has so many different facets. It's never boring. When I try to attract employees, my headline is, "It's not your typical 'TGIF' kind of a job." If you are willing to pay more, you'll attract the best people and that goes a long way. We have set up predictable systems that produce predictable results, which gives my staff a sense of control and lessens stress. It's a fun place to work; we have barbecues, lunches, and dinner cruises. Once, we all went to Las Vegas for some management software training. It's important to invest in your people.

Q: What is the most important attribute that you look for in an employee?

A: Employees should be able to multi-task, and have a sense of humor. You can't be too serious about this business, because

RESIDENTIAL PROPERTY MANAGEMENT, INC.

otherwise you can really get defensive when interacting with tenants and owners.

Q: What are you doing now in your property management business that you wish you had done earlier?

A: I wish I had realized the importance of organization, and putting systems in place for everything. Really, at the beginning, I just didn't know better.

Q: What are some of the biggest mistakes you see new property managers making?

A: New managers focus too much on getting new business rather than setting up the company properly at the beginning. When things are inconsistent and fragmented, it leads to frustration and stress for everyone: owners, tenants and employees. If new managers just take more time initially to organize their business and get support from networking, they'll start out well and have a lot more staying power.

Q: What are some of the biggest challenges that you face?

A: Handling the growth is a challenge. What do you do first? Do you hire staff before you get growth, or hire the staff as you go? In the meantime, there is the challenge of having too much to do already. I'm fairly confident right now that we could absorb another government contract with 150 properties, because of the systems we have set up. I couldn't say that 15 years ago.

> **THE MOST IMPORTANT ATTRIBUTES FOR AN EMPLOYEE ARE A SENSE OF HUMOR AND THE ABILITY TO MULTI-TASK.**

Q: Do you have any tips or tricks that really help you avoid repeating the same mistakes?

A: Getting involved with NARPM, networking, and learning best practices from each other are the best recommendations I can make. I once did an office exchange with a small group of other management companies. We spent two full days at each other's businesses, going through all the systems that we each had in place. That was one of my most valuable experiences.

Q: Describe your best owner.

A: Our best owner's expectations fit our systems. We try to establish upfront that we do things a certain way and, if his expectations don't fit, we'll understand and he'll probably go elsewhere. He also realizes that there are costs and responsibilities associated with being a landlord, and that a tenant is a valued customer who can bring him $10,000-15,000 worth of business on an annual basis. There's always been a sort of adversarial relationship between the landlord and the tenant, but if you set expectations and rules for both of them, it results in better understanding and cooperation from everyone.

Q: What do you find to be the most rewarding aspects of your property management business?

A: It's the flexibility, being able to take off and spend time with my family. I am not married to my business. Also it is very rewarding when an owner, for example, says that we are a godsend.

Q: What would you see as some of the biggest opportunities for new property managers?

A: The best opportunities will come for new property managers who are willing to take the blinders off and be more open to different options for owners and tenants. They shouldn't just focus on leasing and management services, because that's not necessarily what the owners and the tenants need in these troubled economic times. They should be flexible and creative, consider lease options, help structure owner financing, or stay with traditional management. The important thing is fulfilling their clients' needs.

RESIDENTIAL PROPERTY MANAGEMENT, INC.

8

"I attribute my success to luck, hard work, and surrounding myself with good people."

Paul Kaplan, KW Property Management

◆

BACKGROUND

Paul Kaplan is a co-managing director of KW Property Management, based in Florida. Paul's company was established in 2004 and currently has 425 employees in metropolitan areas such as Miami, Naples, Tampa, Daytona, Jacksonville and Orlando. The company oversees approximately 32,000 residential units, and over a million square feet of commercial and office space.

INTERVIEW

Q: How did you get into property management?

A: I was a CPA by trade, but one day, I remember this very well, I was lying in bed and thought, "I should go into property management; how hard could it be?" At the time, my partner Robert White and I, were helping my father's company with condo conversion and management. They gave us office space and we shared the fee that we received. Through that contact, we learned the business from the ground up and quickly became known as property managers for developers. Business just snowballed from there as we added properties every month.

Q: Did you have a mentor at the time?

A: Two key individuals helped us get a start in the business by referring their clients to us, my father's partner, Eduardo Avila, a prominent real-estate broker, and Ronnie Fieldstone, a real estate attorney. Their confidence in us was a tremendous boost; other developers in South Florida appreciated

PAUL KAPLAN

our accounting background.

Q: Were there any educational classes that you have taken that you have found particularly valuable?

A: We must be licensed by the state of Florida and keep that up-to-date, including our CPA and Community Association Manager (CAM) licenses. Our CPA designation gives us a rare advantage in the industry because it's not common among property managers. It adds to our credibility from an accounting and subsidiary responsibility perspective.

Q: How do you keep up with all the laws that affect your property management business?

A: We do in-house training on a weekly basis to keep abreast of current events, and we invite our field employees to participate. Speakers can include property management experts, insurance representatives, attorneys, accountants, and other professionals.

Q: Are there any books that you would recommend, websites, or other educational resources?

A: I personally belong to the American Institute of Certified Public Accountants (AICPA) and the Florida Institute of Certified Public Accounts (FICPA). We're also big advocates of the Community Association Institute (CAI), and the wealth of information they share. They're not a governing body like the state, but they're the primary resource for best practices in the industry.

> **OUR CPA CERTIFICATIONS GIVE US A LOT OF CREDIBILITY IN THE INDUSTRY FROM THE ACCOUNTING PERSPECTIVE. THAT IS SOMETHING THAT VERY FEW PROPERTY MANAGERS HAVE.**

Q: How do you use the Internet to help you with your property management business?

A: Everything we do as a company is electronic and paperless,

KW Property Management

including employee access to our network, and research. The Internet is a tremendous tool; we could not perform the way we do without it.

Q: Do you still use traditional advertising?

A: No, we do a lot of what I would call public relations, educational seminars, newsletters, and speaking engagements.

Q: What do you attribute your success to?

A: Luck, hard work, and surrounding yourself with good people.

Q: When things don't go particularly well, things look kind of bleak, where do you draw your strength and inspiration from?

A: Negative events like losing a client actually motivate me because of the fear. I've always risen to the occasion under pressure; it helps me in the long term because it's like a boost of energy. I can work three times better when I'm nervous!

Q: Do you have any slogans that you personally use or that your company uses?

A: We pride ourselves on our "Triangle Philosophy." If you build your business on these three points of the triangle, you're managing a property correctly: the aesthetics of the property, the financials of the property, and the customer service.

> **COMMUNITY ASSOCIATION INSTITUTE (CAI) IS REALLY THE PRIMARY RESOURCE FOR BEST PRACTICES IN THE INDUSTRY.**

Q: How do you attract and retain the best employees?

A: We do significant recruiting and interview 20 people for every one person we hire. A lot of it is by word of mouth.

Q: What's the most important attribute that you look for in a new employee?

PAUL KAPLAN

A: We'd rather have the "athlete" than somebody with experience. This means we prefer to mold someone into a good manager or a good employee by our standards, as opposed to somebody who's been influenced for years by other people's ways of doing things.

Q: What are you doing now in your property management business that you wish you had done sooner?
A: As entrepreneurs, during our first five years, we were too focused on "growth mode" and not enough on managing the business itself and managing expenses.

Q: What are some of the biggest mistakes that you see new property managers making?
A: Trying to please everybody at once! It's better to admit "I don't know the answer" or to say "Let me get back to you." Then take the time to do the research.

Q: What are some of the biggest challenges that you are facing?
A: Financial markets can be tough. The overall financial health of properties is most challenging, especially managing cash flows, collections and delinquencies.

Q: How do you overcome some of these challenges?
A: We train and encourage our managers to think like business people, to consider their properties and the financials as if that were their own bank account.

Q: Describe for me your best owner/client.
A: The best owners act like owners of a professional business themselves and want to be treated that way, with structure, routine monthly meetings, asset calls on a weekly basis. They let you manage the process.

Q: What have been the most rewarding aspects of your property management business?
A: Watching our growth is incredibly rewarding, not just growth

of the business, but of our employees, people who have been with us from day one becoming leaders and upper management. For example, we had an intern fresh out of college who became manager of one of the largest high-rises in South Florida, in only a couple of years. And he's doing a great job.

Q: What do you see as some of the biggest opportunities for new property managers?

A: One of the best opportunities to break into the business is by seeking out a middle-tier company, not too big or too small, that will provide significant hands-on training. New managers need to learn about operations and financial aspects from the ground up.

> **NEW PROPERTY MANAGERS SHOULD FIND A COMPANY THAT WILL PROVIDE THEM SOME SIGNIFICANT HANDS-ON TRAINING IN OPERATIONS AND FINANCIAL ASPECTS.**

PAUL KAPLAN

"One cannot manage change. One can only be ahead of it."

-Peter F. Drucker

9

"Nothing costs you more than a vacancy."
Mark Kreditor, Get There First Realty

◆

BACKGROUND

Mark Kreditor lives in Dallas, Texas. Mark started his own company, Get There First Realty, in August 1981. He currently has 14 employees and manages over 1500 residential properties. His properties consist of single-family homes, condos, duplexes, multiplexes, and small apartments.

INTERVIEW

Q: How did you get started in property management?

A: After graduating from college I moved to Dallas and got involved with direct marketing. I found I had a passion for advertising outside the box, helping real estate clients find tenants or first-time condo buyers. During the 1980s savings and loan crisis, I turned to the leasing business because buying came to a halt and rentals increased. This is when I discovered the National Association of Residential Property Managers (NARPM). This association gave me the direction I needed to find professionalism, education, and ethics in the industry; I got every certification I could, and began networking with the finest property managers in the country. Later I became national president of NARPM, and I still serve as the national chair for the ethics and professional standards committee.

Q: Did you have a mentor when you first got into property management?

A: Harry Dale was a very important mentor in my life. He always said that if you have something to convey to somebody in a sales presentation, verbal or written, always give three compelling reasons for it, not just one.

Q: How do you keep up on all the new laws that affect your property management business?

A: I'm involved with the Austin legislative committee, which allows me to get a copy of proposed bills, to comment on them to our lobbyists, and to help introduce, amend, or eliminate bad legislation for our industry. I go to workshops, seminars, NARPM chapter meetings, and regional and national conventions.

Q: Are there any recommended books, websites, or other educational resources, that you use on a regular basis that you find valuable?

A: The Texas Real Estate Center offers a very handy landlord/tenant handbook, explaining the various laws in layman's terms. Courses on conflict resolution are critical for property managers! NARPM provides 95% of anything you need, especially if you're managing single-family homes. There's incredible synergy at a NARPM conference; you're in a room with people who do exactly what you do every day.

Q: Do you belong to any other industry associations?

A: I have a Texas real estate license and I belong to the Texas Apartment Association.

Q: How do you use the Internet to help you with your property management business?

A: We have a website for owner/investor information such as newsletters, and one for our customers where we also market our rentals. We provide virtual tours of our properties, place listings on other websites, opt for the better search en-

> **EDUCATIONAL CLASSES ON CONFLICT RESOLUTION ARE CRITICAL FOR PROPERTY MANAGERS.**

gines and use Google AdWords. I also use the Internet for criminal reports, credit reports, and client payments.

Q: Do you do any type of traditional advertising, like in newspapers? If not, what do you do instead?

A: Traditional advertising isn't helpful at all. To be profitable you have to do something truly different, like our door-to-door approach. When a property is available I get all of the neighbors involved with marketing it, helping me to find their new neighbors. We put flyers up at local stores, schools, and break rooms. We use fax and e-mail broadcasting to send out lists of our available properties, which is much cheaper than running a newspaper ad.

> **I TREAT EVERY OWNER AS IF HE IS THE ONLY ONE I HAVE.**

Q: Do you do any PR for your company?

A: PR is absolutely wonderful. Anytime I'm featured in an article, I professionally reprint it with the permission of the publication and send it out to prospective new owners. Most people send out fancy, slick brochures about their company, which costs them a lot of money.

Q: Where do you draw your strength or inspiration from when things are bleak and not going so well for you?

A: I feel great when somebody tells me that he made $100,000 this year because he used my income ideas for tenants or owners; I feel great when I get letters, gifts, and "thank you's". Nothing motivates me more than making a living, especially when I do better, year after year.

Q: What do you attribute your success to?

A: I've built a brand and focused on one very important thing: I treat every owner as if he is the only one I have. I care very much about what people think of me as a business, as a person, as a property manager, as an expert, and as a broker. I will call you back faster, get your check to you much sooner,

MARK KREDITOR

than anybody else; I'm impeccable and meticulous about paperwork. Our policies, leases, understanding of the law, and treatment of the owner or customer are standardized. Those are the keys to success in this business: standardization and consistency. If you build a brand based on that, your business will run as well as it can run, and there's nothing more pleasurable than that.

> I'VE NEVER HAD A LAYOFF. PEOPLE WORK HERE FOREVER.

Q: Are there any slogans that you or your company use?

A: "One call, one solution." "We treat every owner as if he's our only one." "Management, leasing, collections." "Lose the battle. Win the war." "Nothing costs you more than a vacancy." "Work smarter not harder." "Your new lease on life."

Q: How do you attract and retain the best employees?

A: I tell them upfront exactly what's expected, and that this will be the best and last job they will ever have. I want to motivate people to work very, very hard, and to care, more than anything else. We lead by example and I don't ask anybody to do anything differently than I would do. I've never had a layoff; I only grow. People work here forever. It's a very boring, consistent, reliable business.

Q: What's the most important attribute you look for in an employee?

A: I look for good credit and the commitment of 24/7. I check references, but I have the right as an employer to run someone's credit report and I do. I know people have bad things happen to them, and they can explain to me why their credit is not a full picture of who they are; I'll certainly take that into consideration. But if somebody is slow in paying his bills or doesn't pay them at all, he's not going to be as focused as I am on crossing the t's, dotting the i's, and making everyone happy.

Q: What are some of the biggest mistakes that you see new property managers making?

A: They take on too much too soon, and don't get all the educational background they need before accepting their first management account. They think they're going to learn on the job, but it's very hard to do that.

Q: What are some of the biggest challenges that you face?

A: The biggest challenge is getting everybody to like you. Unfortunately, in property management, the only person who likes you is probably the owner. At some point, a tenant may be unhappy about something the owner tells you to do, like raising the rent or postponing an optional repair. I've overcome the challenge by turning it into a positive: I make the owners realize that complaints exemplify how well I'm doing what they want me to do. Any bad things tenants may say about me are exactly the reasons why owners should want to hire me.

> **WHEN I HIRE NEW EMPLOYEES, I LOOK FOR PEOPLE WITH GOOD CREDIT AND THE COMMITMENT OF 24/7.**

Q: How do you deal with difficult tenant issues and tenant conflicts?

A: We only speak in the third person. Most conversations we have with a tenant start off with "I understand, but the owner said..." We're never really a party to the lease, so we're held harmless in the management agreements and avoid lawsuits.

Q: Describe your best client and your best tenant.

A: My best client really listens to me, reads my newsletters, and believes that I have his best interest in mind by helping him lose the least amount of money; my clients pick their own tenants as well. My best tenant always tells me the truth, even when it's not what I want to hear – for example, about

MARK KREDITOR

possible problems on his application. The best tenants are respectful, they understand the lease terms, and they listen. Many times we can't get a word in!

Q: What have been the most rewarding aspects of your property management business?

A: There is nothing that makes me more energized and recharged than meeting and teaching people who want to get into this business. There's nothing I enjoy more than learning from students who ask the same questions in different ways.

> **MY BEST CLIENT REALLY LISTENS TO ME, READS MY NEWSLETTERS, AND BELIEVES THAT I'M GOING TO HELP HIM LOSE THE LEAST AMOUNT OF MONEY.**

GET THERE FIRST REALTY

10

"The most rewarding aspect of property management is working with people and students."
William J. Levy, CPM, Best Management Onward Campus

◆

BACKGROUND

William J. Levy, CPM, lives in Madison, Wisconsin and is the CEO of Best Management Onward Campus (BMOC). BMOC has over 300 employees in Wisconsin, Illinois, Philadelphia, and Indiana. They manage six properties with over 3,000 beds, specializing in student apartments and housing. William is a national faculty member with the Institute of Real Estate Management (IREM). Throughout his career, William has managed student housing in almost every state in the U.S.

INTERVIEW

Q: How did you get into property management, and did you have a mentor at the time?

A: While putting myself through college I became an assistant general manager of a building with 824 beds at the University of South Florida. I was a marketing major and never thought I'd end up in property management! Jim Laduwa was my mentor, employer, and my best friend when I worked for Northwest Mutual Life Insurance; he became head of their real estate department. He was not only my mentor for property management, but also for my life in general.

Q: What educational classes have you taken, that you have found particularly valuable to help you in property management?

A: I just sat on a board at the University of Wisconsin (Stout) and they will implement a four-year degree in property management in January 2010. Only a handful of colleges in the country actually offer such a degree. The property management education offered through the IREM is so valuable; I earned my Certified Property Manager (CPM) designation there. I took real estate courses in college, but nothing comes even close to the amazing experience I've had with the IREM.

Q: Are there any associations that you belong to that are industry-specific?

A: I belong to IREM, the local Wisconsin Realtor's Board, and the National Realtor's Association.

Q: How do you use the Internet and how has it helped you in property management?

A: The Internet is the ultimate tool in our business today, though you have to be careful because it's also a potential vehicle for people to damage your reputation. However, we do use Craigslist, Facebook, and Twitter, and offer virtual tours of our properties on our website. The signs at our rentals display a code that people can punch into their cell phones, and bring up all the information about the property. Our tenants can request work orders and pay their rent online.

> THE UNIVERSITY OF WISCONSIN (STOUT) IS IMPLEMENTING A FOUR-YEAR DEGREE IN PROPERTY MANAGEMENT.

Q: What do you attribute your success to?

A: Timing, being at the right place at the right time and having the right answers. I'm good at problem solving and that certainly helps in this industry.

Q: When things aren't going so well, where do you draw your strength and inspiration from?

A: I roll up my sleeves and work extra hard. Eventually the good times come back, but not easily. At the end of the day, I'm the one who's going to pick myself up and make things happen. I have a great team of people that I keep in mind, because if I fall, they'll fall with me.

Q: What are you doing now in property management that you wish you had done sooner?

A: There is nothing better than owning your own company. You really get to create change, and I love it.

Q: What are some of the biggest mistakes that you see new property managers making?

A: Some will tell an owner anything to make him happy or to get the account. They'll use finance people just out of college to write $20 million pro forma, who don't know anything about how the property will actually operate. It's very dangerous to have people without the proper experience and depth, making very big presentations to investors. I tell my clients that somewhere up at the top of the company, someone should have some gray hair!

> I ATTRIBUTE MY SUCCESS TO BEING AT THE RIGHT PLACE AT THE RIGHT TIME AND HAVING THE RIGHT ANSWERS.

WILLIAM J. LEVY

Q: What are some of the biggest challenges you face and how do you overcome them?

A: I have a lot of best friends with too many vacancies, half-empty buildings. You have to figure out how to make your product fit the demographic of the end user. For example, our younger tenants typically want things done "right now." They're used to turning on the computer and getting entertainment, TV, and music instantaneously. So we try to accommodate them by offering our surveys online and holding town halls because they like to provide input into their community.

Q: What's been the most rewarding aspect of your property management business?

A: Working with people, especially the students. I love people.

Q: What do you see as some of the biggest opportunities for new property managers?

A: People are choosing where to live based on a lifestyle, and want to know what services you provide. You have to consider those lifestyles and what your product can give to the community. I've put flat screen plasma TVs in the rooms – the "wow" effect has been amazing. People ask things like, "You have a beautiful gym, do you give massages?" One way to provide a service is to work with local resources like schools or licensing agencies. For example, I've partnered with a massage school to have their students give volunteer hours of massages at my property. That in turn, helps the students get their certification and license. It's been very popular with my tenants.

> **THERE IS NOTHING BETTER THAN OWNING YOUR OWN COMPANY AND I LOVE IT.**

11

"If you keep it clean, green and well maintained, they will come."
Dori Locke, Right On Coaching and Consulting

◆

BACKGROUND

Dori Locke lives in Tucson, Arizona. She worked for the MC Company and was president and managing partner of Tucson Realty & Trust Co. Management Services, LLC (TRTMS). Tucson Realty and Trust was a full service fee management company that managed over 700 single-family homes, 4,000 multi-family apartment units, almost two million square feet of commercial space (retail, office, and some light industrial), and over 6,000 homes in association management. Dori has over 25 years of experience in property management, and currently owns her own consulting company, Right On Coaching and Consulting.

INTERVIEW

Q: How did you get into property management?

A: I was just 18 years old, wanting to get out of working retail at the local mall. A girlfriend of mine was a leasing agent and she talked me into checking it out. I started as a part-time leasing agent.

Q: Did you have a mentor when you got started in property management?

A: It didn't take me long to identify people I respected, who had been in the industry for a while. One of my first mentors was Dee Holmes. I worked with her to establish some skill sets that helped me in my career.

Q: What educational classes have you taken that have proven to be particularly valuable to you?

A: I received my Certified Apartment Manager (CAM) and Certified Apartment Property Supervisor (CAPS) designations from the National Apartment Association (NAA). I also have my Certified Property Manager (CPM) designation from the Institute of Real Estate Management (IREM).

Q: How do you keep up with all the new laws that affect your property management business?

A: The professional associations like NAA and IREM are the best way, and membership is a virtual necessity. For managing single-family homes there is the National Association of Residential Property Managers (NARPM) and for commercial property managers, the Building Owners and Managers Association (BOMA). I've been on the board of the Arizona Multihousing Association (AMA) for many years. I'm also a voting delegate to the NAA, and a past chapter president for IREM in Tucson.

> **WE CREATED COMMUNITY PAGES ON FACEBOOK FOR EACH OF OUR PROPERTIES, WHICH HELPED FROM A BRANDING STANDPOINT.**

Q: Are there any books, websites, or other educational resources that you have found to be particularly valuable to you?

A: I'd recommend *Outliers* and *Blink*, both by Malcolm Gladwell. My current coaching consulting company does training for people in the property management industry, and I've given talks on motivation to organizations like the Portland Apartment Association and the AMA.

Q: How has the Internet helped you in your property management business?

A: We've used various apartment magazine websites, Craigslist and Twitter. We also created community pages on Facebook for each of our properties, which helped from a branding standpoint.

RIGHT ON COACHING AND CONSULTING

Q: What are your thoughts on traditional advertising?

A: Most of the traditional advertising media are positioning themselves to somehow embrace the Internet, but I find that the local newspapers, the magazines, and the apartment guides are still viable and vibrant.

Q: What do you attribute your success to in property management?

A: I emulated the successful people around me, and was willing to take on any and all jobs because then I became a key resource for everyone. I also credit the industry designations I obtained.

> **I WAS SUCCESSFUL BECAUSE I EMULATED THE SUCCESSFUL PEOPLE AROUND ME.**

Q: When things don't go so well, where do you draw your strength and inspiration from?

A: I just take a little time with myself every day to get grounded in what I want to create, and what I want the day to look like. It's not in what's happening to me, it's how I deal with what's happening.

Q: Any slogans that you or your company have?

A: "If you keep it clean, green and well maintained, they will come." "Solutions are all around me."

Q: How do you attract and retain the best employees?

A: I like to counsel people to figure out what their strengths and weaknesses are, and to learn what they just love to do, what is important to them. Then I help them find a position within our organization that serves those things.

Q: What's the most important attribute you look for?

A: I like people who want to learn, to help, and to do; people who are hungry. I like it when a prospective employee interviews me, when he wants to know what my company is all

DORI LOCKE

about! He's trying to figure out why he would want to work here.

Q: What are some of the biggest mistakes that you see new property managers making?

A: The biggest mistake I see new managers make is trying to handle it all and not properly delegating. It's difficult, but very important.

Q: What are some of the biggest challenges that you faced when you were a property manager?

A: Separating my personal and professional life was a real challenge.

Q: Do you have any tips or tricks to avoid making the same mistakes?

A: I keep myself educated and informed about changes in the industry. I realize that I don't have all the answers, and try to stay open to others' ideas and solutions. That includes allowing my entire team to have input into problem solving and discussions.

Q: Describe for me your best client.

A: My best client is really engaged but not to the point of always being at the property, bothering me and my staff; he takes responsibility for his investment and pays his bills on time. When I meet with a new potential client, I interview him as much as he does me. If we're not pulling in the same direction, it can be a miserable process for everyone.

> **THE BIGGEST MISTAKE I SEE NEW MANAGERS MAKE IS TRYING TO HANDLE IT ALL AND NOT PROPERLY DELEGATING.**

Q: What's been the most rewarding aspect of being in the property management business?

A: It's most rewarding to see that a resident really loves the home I am providing for him.

Q: What are some of the biggest opportunities you see for new property managers?

A: There will always be opportunities in the property management industry. One thing I love about it is that I can live anywhere in the world. Where is there a place that doesn't have rental housing? I can find a job anywhere!

> **WHEN I INTERVIEW A NEW POTENTIAL CLIENT, I DO AS MUCH INTERVIEWING OF HIM AS HE DOES OF ME.**

DORI LOCKE

"When you're finished changing,
you're finished."
-Benjamin Franklin

12

"Build a strong team and set high expectations with accountability."

Tracey Logan, Holland Residential

◆

BACKGROUND

Tracey Logan lives in Denver, Colorado. She has been with Holland Residential since May 2006, and is currently a vice president and partner responsible for operations in Arizona and Colorado. The company has 450 employees and manages 60 residential, multi-family properties.

INTERVIEW

Q: How did you get into property management?

A: When I was in college I worked for my sister's friend as a part-time leasing consultant at the small community she managed. It worked well with my school schedule, I really enjoyed it, and the rest is history.

Q: Did you have a mentor when you started?

A: Yes, I worked with Rhonda Hansch for eight years; she taught me a tremendous amount. She loved training and coaching, and I was exposed to things that a lot of property managers aren't. Rhonda took a pretty big leap of faith with me when she made me manager of a 500-unit apartment community, with a staff of 14, at the age of 21. That was a big responsibility for that age level.

Q: Any educational classes that you've taken that you have found to be particularly valuable?

A: I'd recommend getting at least a bachelor's degree. It's not absolutely necessary, and you can move up through the industry without it, but at the higher levels of management it's an advantage. The Apartment Association of Metro Denver (AAMD), the National Apartment Association (NAA), and the Institute of Real Estate Management (IREM), all offer great classes like the leasing course and the Certified Apartment Manager course. You can now take management courses at a lot of colleges too.

Q: You mentioned the importance of a college degree; any particular major or focus with that college degree?

A: It's been extremely beneficial to have a business degree. I've done a lot of marketing, advertising, people development, leadership, accounting, and finance.

Q: How do you keep up with all of the new laws that impact your property management business?

A: The apartment association does a great job of keeping us in the loop on a regular basis with notifications, and our attorneys send out detailed newsletters to make sure we know about any changes that affect us.

Q: Any recommended books, websites, or other educational resources that you'd recommend?

A: *Good to Great* by Jim Collins is an excellent book to move your business forward. *Moneyball* by Michael M. Lewis is really interesting and contains a lot of different management styles and ideas.

Q: Which industry associations do you belong to?

A: We belong to the AAMD, the NAA and the National Multi-Housing Council. In all of the states where we do business, we're a part of the local associations, which tie in with the national ones and do a great job of providing education on sales training, maintenance, and other topics. They also provide networking opportunities, like an annual trade show that lets you seek out new vendors and new types of businesses. We all share best practices and ideas, and get a real sense of community within our industry.

Q: How has the Internet helped you?

A: Most of our leads and leases are Internet-based, which has significantly reduced our advertising expenses and substantially broadened our renter base. From a recruiting perspective, the Internet has made it easier to see applicants from all over the country and fill jobs faster.

> **INDUSTRY ASSOCIATIONS ARE A GREAT PLACE TO SHARE BEST PRACTICES AND IDEAS, AND TO LEARN ABOUT SUCCESSFUL PRACTICES OTHER COMPANIES ARE IMPLEMENTING.**

Q: Do you use any of the social networking tools in your property management business?

A: All of our websites are connected to Twitter. I have Facebook pages for two student-based properties in Arizona, that's working fairly well, with an intentionally targeted demographic. We have not done specific advertising on Facebook yet.

Q: Do you still use traditional advertising, like the newspaper?

A: I'm known in my company as "Internet Only Tracey." I think I have one property with a print ad right now, which saves me a lot on advertising. Occasionally we advertise in the Arizona State University paper, during the student housing fair.

Q: What about PR, do you use TV or radio to promote your company?

A: Last year the CEO of our company was interviewed on TV about our "Job Loss Program," which is a job loss protection program for renters. Positive PR is always a win and you should take advantage of it. Regular press releases are another inexpensive way to market.

TRACEY LOGAN

Q: Can you say a little bit more about the Job Loss Program?

A: We recognized that we need to change when the economy does. With significant numbers of people unemployed or worried about getting laid off, we decided to offer this job loss protection program. If a tenant is laid off after renewing a lease or signing a new one, he can be released from his contract. Our occupancy levels have been outperforming those of our competitors in large part because of the success of this program.

> **THE BEST EMPLOYEE IS SOMEONE WHO LIKES TO BE AROUND PEOPLE, HAS A POSITIVE ATTITUDE, AND WANTS TO LEARN.**

Q: What do you attribute your success to in property management?

A: Initially, I worked really hard and learned as much as I could; I had the advantage of a mentor who took the time to coach and educate me. Now, building a strong team and setting high expectations with accountability are important. And we always remember that the customers are our "bread and butter."

Q: Where do you draw your strength or inspiration from when things aren't going so well?

A: When the economy is really tough, it's an opportunity to learn the most, to evaluate what you're doing, reflect on what was successful and what was not, and apply the lessons learned. Business runs in cycles, so it's important to define a solid business strategy that will take you through each cycle, and will enable you to have the most impact now.

Q: How do you attract and retain the best employees?

A: We look for people with initiative, who really want to get involved, take the time to learn and gain experience. Then we first and foremost promote from within, because you're going to be better off: you already know what your employees'

HOLLAND RESIDENTIAL

strengths and weaknesses are, and they already know what the company culture is like. We encourage a positive work environment that balances having fun with getting the job done. We hold our employees accountable for meeting or exceeding expectations, but we also make sure we recognize people when they've achieved their goals.

Q: What's the most important attribute that you look for in a new employee?

A: We want someone who likes to be around people, has a positive attitude, and wants to learn.

Q: What are you doing now in your property management business that you feel you should have started sooner?

A: Recently we started doing some tenant surveys to rate a number of areas of customer satisfaction. The feedback we've received has been eye-opening in some instances! We should have done this earlier and more frequently.

Q: What are some of the biggest mistakes you see new property managers making?

A: They may forget that we extend a really personal experience by providing someone a home. Our residents need a clean, well-maintained home they can be proud of, and they deserve good customer service, which managers sometimes forget. New managers also tend to hire people who are like them,

> **TRY TO HIRE PEOPLE WHO ARE BRIGHTER THAN YOU.**

have similar personalities, but diversity can be very beneficial to the team. Surround yourself with a variety of personalities and skill sets that are different, yet complementary. And if at all possible, hire people who are brighter than you.

Q: What are some of the biggest challenges you face and how do you overcome some of those challenges?

A: The challenge of finding qualified renters has caused us to

TRACEY LOGAN

adjust our resident qualifying criteria. For example, we now exclude foreclosures as a disqualifier. We decided not to consider foreclosure as a negative mark on credit background checks, to help people who have experienced a one-time problem obtain housing more easily. Another solution has been our Job Loss Program.

Q: Any tips or tricks that you have to avoid repeating the same mistake?

A: I always ask myself what I could have done differently to create the desired outcome, and reflect on why a success was a success, and what led to shortfalls.

Q: Describe for me your best owner/client, and also your best resident.

A: We align ourselves with investors or partners whose strategies and cultures match our company's. My best residents care about their community and their apartment home, let management know if there's something wrong with the property, and of course they pay their rent on time.

Q: What have been the most rewarding aspects of your property management business?

A: I love the dynamic nature of the business; it's constantly changing so there's no monotony. We get to dabble in a variety of different business lines and utilize different skills: customer service, finance, accounting, marketing, and human resources. Sometimes we're like a bartender or a counselor to our residents!

Q: What do you see as some of the biggest opportunities for new property managers?

A: As the economy turns around, there will be plenty of new opportunities for growth and advancement. There will also be more ways for connecting with people via social media and the Internet, which I don't think is fully utilized yet in our industry.

13

"Listening is such a huge part of our business."
Mark Mascia, Mascia Management

◆

BACKGROUND

Mark Mascia lives in New York, NY. He is the president and CEO of Mascia Management, established in 2008. Mark's company has five employees and manages 15 residential properties consisting of one to 30 units each.

INTERVIEW

Q: How did you get into property management?

A: I started out in real estate investment and development, but most of the people on my team didn't really understand the assets in the true operating sense. We realized it was important to maintain a personal knowledge base and relationship with our properties, so we started the property management company.

Q: Did you have a mentor at the time?

A: I have had lots of mentors but the most important one was Ed Peete. I'm basically just following his buying and management model.

Q: How do you keep up with local, state, and federal laws relative to property management?

A: We use LinkedIn a lot. We use it to connect to other property managers and partcipate with the discussion forums on pending legislation. We also read most of the trade journals, receive e-newsletters from our attorneys, and occasionally attend new classes that the city offers.

Q: Are there any specific books, websites, or other educational resources that you'd recommend?

A: I feel very strongly that customer service is lacking in our industry; a lot of people don't really see the value of it or necessarily understand it. So I make all of our people read books like *Nuts!: Southwest Airlines' Crazy Recipe for Business and Personal Success* by Kevin & Jackie Freiberg, and *How to Win Friends and Influence People* by Dale Carnegie. It's all about how to make people happy and feel like they're being heard.

> **WE USE LINKEDIN TO CONNECT TO OTHER PROPERTY MANAGERS AND TO VARIOUS GROUPS THAT HAVE DISCUSSION FORUMS.**

Q: Are you involved with any of the industry associations?

A: We're joining the National Apartment Association (NAA). Mainly because of the green certification that they offer. I belong to the Urban Land Institute and the United States Green Building Council; they're quite helpful and offer high-level education opportunities.

Q: How do you use the Internet to help you with your property management business?

A: We try to leverage technology as much as possible to increase our efficiency. This allows us to spend more time doing things that technology can't do, like dealing with customer issues. We hired an in-house public relations person to start a blog and manage our Facebook and Twitter accounts. Many of our current and potential clients are very sophisticated and intelligent investors, and these tools provide them with helpful information and tips.

Q: Do you do any traditional advertising?

A: We do some traditional advertising, just to make sure we have a comprehensive marketing plan in a difficult business environment. But in all honesty, it probably hasn't been very

MASCIA MANAGEMENT

beneficial for us.

Q: Do you do any PR for your company?

A: It's extremely important, and it's the main reason we hired an in-house public relations person. Clients have told us that our PR convinced them that we were the right company for them.

Q: What do you attribute your success to?

A: It was very difficult to give up a good salary and a stable job to start my own company. But I never gave up, and the support I've had from family and friends made all the difference.

> **I ATTRIBUTE MY SUCCESS TO NEVER GIVING UP.**

Q: When things aren't going so well, where do you draw your strength and inspiration from?

A: I'll definitely do more to help other people that rely on me, than I will do to help myself. All I have to do for strength and inspiration is think about not letting my family down, or about the people who work for me and rely on me to keep things going.

Q: Do you have any slogans, either for you personally or for your company?

A: "I will either find a way or make one." Lots of times people say, "That's not possible," or "You can't do that." "Nothing is impossible, you just have to figure out a way."

Q: How do you attract and retain the best employees?

A: I usually find my best employees through referrals from people I trust; then I follow through and retain those employees with trust, responsibility, and appreciation. I don't micromanage; I let people do their job as autonomously as possible, and ask me for help when they need it. Saying "thanks" for a good job, or a more award-driven appreciation, is so

MARK MASCIA

important.

Q: What's the most important attribute that you look for in an employee?

A: We look for people who are intelligent and can solve customer problems while considering the ramifications of their solution. We want people to think confidently about the situation and not feel pressured to make an instant decision.

Q: What are you doing now in your property management business that you wish you had done sooner?

A: No matter how successful or how happy you are, there will always be attrition and changes in the market to consider. I should have realized that and spent more time growing my business rather than running it. Never stop growing your business.

Q: What are some of the biggest mistakes that you see new property managers making?

A: Property managers need to have the patience to really listen to their customers; too many of them think they know how a conversation will go and cut customers off with a "no." Sometimes people simply need to be heard, even if it's a complaint, and a lot of problems can be resolved just by listening. That's customer service, and there isn't enough focus on it.

Q: What are some of the biggest challenges that you face?

A: The biggest challenge is educating some landlords and managers about the value of technology and environment-friendly innovations in the industry. Especially in New York City and the tri-state area, sadly, nothing has changed in 30 years! We have to demonstrate that you can be lower cost because you're more efficient, not because you provide a lower level of service. That efficiency is

> **NOTHING IS IMPOSSIBLE, YOU JUST HAVE TO FIGURE OUT A WAY.**

based on being educated about the changes in our industry and using them to the best advantage.

Q: How do you communicate your company's value proposition to your prospective customers?

A: We listen and tailor our services to their needs. Cost savings is usually the most important factor for the majority of our clients who are smaller property owners. When the market rebounds and becomes more stable, they'll be less interested in cutting expenses for short-term gain, and will invest in retention and quality of service. When it comes to marketing, we'll do what is known as "split testing" on different ad approaches. For example, we'll do one ad that is totally green-focused, another that's technologically focused, and one that might be totally price-focused. Then we'll use the method that proves most effective for us.

Q: Any tips or tricks that you have that have helped you avoid repeating the same mistakes?

A: Our board of advisors consists of members from all aspects of the industry: a lawyer, a banker, a property management technology specialist, and others with experience in their specific fields. They provide a fresh "outsider's perspective" that is incredibly valuable to us.

Q: Describe for me your best owner.

A: Our best owner wants us to completely manage his property, down to renovation work with tax incentives and a huge payoff in the long-term; he has the long view on real estate and doesn't demand that we cut expenses to the bare minimum. That approach doesn't benefit the owner in the long-run, or the tenants. A well-maintained property attracts good tenants who appreciate it, are proud of it, and take good care of it.

Q: What have been some of the most rewarding aspects of your business?

MARK MASCIA

A: It's very rewarding to take management of a failing property, implement a comprehensive plan, and turn it around to the point of profitability. A lot of owners have come to us recently in dire straits. Our teams for collections and tenant screening, help solve existing cash flow problems and prevent future ones with future tenants. It's great to help people avoid going into foreclosure and losing an asset.

Q: What are some of the biggest opportunities that you see for new property managers?

A: Environmentally focused or "green" building is not a fad, it's here to stay, and in the next 10 to 20 years — it will change the way we operate and live in buildings. Whether it's new information systems or the new way we buy power, it's so important. Too many people are still behind the times on these issues.

MASCIA MANAGEMENT

14

"If it was easy, everyone would be doing it."
Mia Melle, West Coast Property Specialists, Inc.

◆

BACKGROUND

Mia Melle lives in Chino, California. She formally established West Coast Property Specialists, Inc. in 2003. Mia is the president of operations for the property management division, whose website can be found at www.RentToday.us. The company manages about 1,000 single-family residences throughout Southern California (Los Angeles to San Diego).

INTERVIEW

Q: How did you get into property management?

A: We got into property management a little bit by accident. Initially we planned to just invest in real estate ourselves, and came across a prominent investment club in our region. We gave a presentation on property management to this organization, and the funny part of it is we had never done property management before — ever! But it must have sounded good, because that's what allowed us to start growing our property management clientele from that point forward.

Q: When you got started, did you have a mentor?

A: We really didn't have a mentor, which I think worked to our benefit. We had to learn the laws and everything else ourselves, but without a mentor we didn't start out with any bad habits, and we innovated with our own new ideas.

Q: How did you learn about all the laws related to property management?

A: The state of California requires you to be a real estate broker if you're going into property management. The process involves college courses, becoming a full-time agent and, after two years, a broker. But the most valuable education is experience, and trial and error. Reading the Wall Street Journal and talking with investors about what they're buying, probably gives us the best education we can get on a daily basis.

Q: Who do you use for your credit checks?

A: We get credit reports on our prospective tenants directly from the three main credit bureaus: Experian, Trans Union, and Equifax.

Q: How have you used the Internet to help you with your business?

A: We consider ourselves to be an Internet company, just as much as we are a property management company. We do all of our marketing on the Internet, and advertise our rentals on at least 25 different websites, with the purpose of bringing traffic to our own site through links. I design our website myself; we do all our own site development in-house with an IT department, and process our rental applications online. We get up to 3,000 unique visitors to our website, www.RentToday.us, every day. Ninety percent of our owners and tenants find us this way.

> **WE JUST HIRED A SOCIAL MEDIA PERSON TO REALLY START FOCUSING ON USING THESE TOOLS TO HELP OUR BUSINESS.**

Q: Have you gotten involved in any of the online social networks to help your business?

A: We just hired a social media person to optimize network tools and gain additional business. We're on Facebook, Twitter, and LinkedIn, and we are currently working on our own blog.

Q: Do you do any type of traditional newspaper advertising?

A: We haven't done any traditional advertising for about five years; 98% of our tenants and owners will start by going to the Internet.

Q: Do you do anything with PR to get media attention?

A: We take an active approach in the community, attend events that will be written about in local newspapers, and issue regular press releases on company news. We also make ourselves available as "industry experts" to reporters writing articles on the real estate industry.

> **IF YOU DO EVERYTHING EVERY SINGLE DAY CONSISTENTLY, YOU ARE GOING TO GET BETTER AND BETTER AT IT NO MATTER WHAT.**

Q: What do you attribute your success to?

A: We decided early on that we were going to focus on one thing, property management, and do it well. At first we tried to do everything for our investors, but we found it just takes away from your core business. We've focused on asset and property management for the last seven years, and consistency is the key. If you're consistent, you're going to get better at what you do, no matter what.

Q: When things don't go particularly well and get a little bleak, where do you draw your strength or inspiration from?

A: I work with my husband Damien Melle, the CEO of our company. He is always the rock, always very positive, and I look to him when it seems like everything is falling apart. He'll take me to a conference room and give me a pep talk, and then I'm good.

Q: Are there any slogans that come to mind that help you overcome challenges?

A: "If it was easy, everyone would be doing it." Damien has told

MIA MELLE

me that throughout the years. Owning and running your own business is not easy; there are so many things that frustrate you or get you stressed out. There are benefits, but in order to get those benefits you have to go through the hard times.

Q: How many employees do you have and how do you retain and attract the best ones?

A: We have about 40 employees, and try to provide a great working environment that's casual and fun. Our office is open and bright, with background music and a very high energy running through it. The staff members get to dress more casually than in most office environments, and a couple of them even bring their dogs to work. We offer competitive wages, health benefits, vacations, and a monthly bonus program based on goal achievement.

Q: What is the most important attribute you look for in a new employee?

A: I want someone who exudes energy, enthusiasm, and a good personality; we want our company culture to be energetic and fun. I also look for stability and reliability.

Q: What are you doing now in your property management business that you feel you should have started sooner?

A: We should have focused more on marketing our business. We've always been really great at marketing and leasing our properties, but we put marketing our own company on the back burner. Now we send out weekly newsletters and emails to our clients, and we use public relations more than direct advertising. If someone says something good about you, that's always much better than you saying it about yourself.

Q: What are some of the biggest mistakes you see new property managers making?

A: New managers need to understand marketing. I shop all my competition weekly just to see what they are doing, where and how. Often they are not doing any marketing, even on their own websites. Their sites may be hard to navigate, have wrong information, or be over-complicated. Marketing should be simple and easy for potential clients to understand.

Q: What are some of the biggest challenges that you are facing?

A: Foreclosures are our biggest challenge right now. Owners who bought several homes a few years ago as an investment, are now deciding to let them go into foreclosure. It is very upsetting to our tenants if we have to relocate them. However, in California, the process takes almost a year, and a new law keeps leases from being voided due to foreclosure. This is some comfort to tenants, knowing they can at least ride out the term of their lease.

Q: Tell me about one of the funniest or most bizarre incidents you've encountered with a tenant or client?

A: Just yesterday we had someone who wanted us to manage his rental property, but in the lease, he wanted to stipulate that the tenants were not allowed to walk on the carpet. We encounter the most ridiculous things that you could ever think of.

Q: Describe your best client.

A: Our best client understands why he hired us, trusts us, and lets us do our job. He doesn't try to micromanage us or question us at every turn. The majority of our clients are definitely like that; they want us to handle it, get it done, and do it right.

Q: What have been the most rewarding aspects of your property management business?

A: It's rewarding to be able to create and innovate, see things come to life. I'm lucky to use my creative side working on our website and designing company literature. When you own your own management company, you have the freedom of

MIA MELLE

being your own boss.

Q: What do you see as some of the biggest opportunities for new property managers?

A: The real estate climate is prime for anyone in the property management field. There are more new opportunities out there than ever before, with banks taking large portfolios of foreclosed properties and converting them into rentals, or hedge funds buying up residential housing as an investment model. These businesses need professional, reliable property management companies to provide an infrastructure and handle it all on a daily basis. This is a huge opportunity for property managers.

> **THE REAL ESTATE CLIMATE IS PRIME FOR ANYONE IN THE PROPERTY MANAGEMENT FIELD. THERE ARE SO MANY NEW OPPORTUNITIES OUT THERE THAT WERE NOT AVAILABLE BEFORE.**

West Coast Property Specialists, Inc.

15

"You have to be able to relate to people at all different levels."

Matt Middel, Middel Realty

◆

BACKGROUND

Matt Middel lives in Fort Collins, Colorado. He works for Middel Realty, a property management company started by his grandfather in 1975. Matt has over 20 years of experience in the industry and manages hundreds of residential rentals.

Matt's key to being a successful property manager:
"Long hours. Most folks who succeed put in that extra 10%. The 10% pays off, and then they put in another 10%. You just keep going. I love to work. I have been doing this since I was five years old – trimming bushes with my Dad – and I just enjoy it."

INTERVIEW

Q: How did you get into property management?

A: Middel Realty is a third generation company. In our family, you either chose to become a part of it or chose to move into a different field. After exploring those other fields I found that I prefer doing property management.

Q: Did you have a mentor?

A: Yes, my Grandpa (John Middel) and Dad (Mark Middel). Dad was always a practical salesman. He was honest and had a lot of integrity. Susan Waterman, our office manager, has taught me so much about office work. It's been great to learn so much from her.

Q: Any educational classes that you have taken that have proven to be valuable to you?

A: I recommend the National Association of Residential Property Managers (NARPM) and their classes, which teach how to deal with owners and tenants. The experience level of the members ranges from just starting out to many years in the business; it's very much a collaborative spirit in that organization. Make sure to get a real estate license, and stay up-to-date on continuing education to be familiar with property management law. There are a lot of loopholes, and you don't want to lose your license.

Q: And what's the easiest way to keep up on all the relevant laws?

A: You have to be self-motivated; NARPM will help with this, especially when you are just starting out. I keep up with all the real estate news, consult our state's real estate regulatory agency websites, and use an attorney for my management contracts.

Q: Are there any books, websites, or other educational resources that you would recommend?

A: I've been reading *Taxes 2009 for Dummies* (by Eric Tyson, MBA, Margaret A. Munro, EA, David J. Silverman, EA) for the last couple of weeks, just because it's interesting.

Q: Has the Internet helped you at all and how do you use the Internet?

A: I use the Internet for advertising and for background checks. The Internet can either help you or hurt you because the entire world will see it, including your competition. Make sure your information is right the first time, well-written, and professional, because it could stay there forever. Monitor your competition's website or real estate advertising as well.

> **OUR BIGGEST PROBLEM WITH THE INTERNET HAS BEEN FRAUD. PEOPLE HAVE BEEN TAKING OUR LISTINGS AND PUTTING THEM ON CRAIGSLIST IN THEIR OWN NAME.**

MIDDEL REALTY

Our biggest problem with the Internet has been fraud. People have been taking our listings and putting them on Craigslist in their own name.

Q: Are there any tools that you use that you have found to be useful?

A: It takes time and effort to make sure your various website listings look good. Take some classes! I'm learning HTML, JavaScript and web page design. If you're going to use an advertising agency, find one that is going to be around for the long haul, not just there one day and gone the next.

> **TRADITIONAL NEWSPAPER LISTINGS ARE TOO EXPENSIVE AND NOT PRODUCTIVE.**

Q: Have you used any of the social media sites such as Facebook, Twitter or LinkedIn? If so, have they been useful to you?

A: I'm currently testing an ad on Facebook. Am I expecting great things? No. I think Facebook is just a fad, and will eventually go away like MySpace. You could use it if you want to target college students; great for now, but you need something solid.

Q: Do you find traditional advertising helpful, like newspaper advertising?

A: Traditional newspaper listings are too expensive and not productive. You have to limit yourself to "3BR/2.5BA House for Rent". That little sentence right there will cost you $200 for an ad in the paper. With a website like NorthernColoradoRentals.com, it costs me a mere $9.95 per ad per week.

Q: What do you attribute your success to?

A: Long hours. Most people who succeed put in that extra 10%. The 10% pays off, and then they put in another 10%. And you just keep going. I love to work. Laying out the ground rules with the tenants has also contributed to my success.

MATT MIDDEL

Q: When you hire employees, what do you look for?

A: Employees should have integrity, critical thinking skills, and excellent interaction skills. They need to be quick-witted because they are going to get phone calls from people who are absolutely belligerent. They have to have a sense of humor, but still be able to remind people of our policies.

Q: What are you doing now in your property management business that you should have started doing sooner?

A: I wish we had put more graphics in our ads, to make them stand out. We're doing that now, but we should have done it sooner. You have to do whatever you can to make yourself stand out from the competition.

Q: Do you have a personal or company slogan that you use?

A: Our slogan on our website is, "We do business on a handshake." I follow everything with a piece of paper legally, because that's what you need to do, that's just the nature of the beast. But my word is my bond, so I will honor my word 100%. You can choose to violate yours, and that's your choice.

Q: What are the biggest mistakes you see new property managers making?

A: Some new managers try to grow too big, too fast, so they can earn money and get out. If you're going to make a business of it, it should be for the long run. Build a reputation, be fair and honest with everybody, don't get defensive on the little things, make sure you know the law, and the business will come. Today, the courts almost always side with the tenants on issues, so the landlord should always be informed. Talk to your fellow property managers for advice, and join associations like NARPM.

Q: What are some of the biggest challenges that you currently face, and what do you do to overcome these challenges?

A: If you live in a regulated state like Colorado, you have to know the laws and regulations. It's just a part of doing business. If you document everything and have good policies in place to govern everything you do, you will make it through okay. We cover all that in our policy manual. For example, our policy with bankruptcies is that if an applicant has had a bankruptcy in the last two years, he must pay twice the normal security deposit; however it can be paid over a 9-10 month period.

> **THE BEST TENANT IS ONE WHO PAYS THE RENT ON TIME, AND IF THERE IS A NEEDED REPAIR, THEY LET YOU KNOW ABOUT IT**

Q: What's one of the funniest or most bizarre incidents you've encountered from a tenant or an owner?

A: All of our properties have a "no pet" policy. One day we went to do a repair in someone's place and there were three turkeys penned up in the kitchen! We reminded the tenant of our "no pet" policy, and he said, "No pets. Food!"

Q: Describe your best tenant.

A: The best tenant is one who is not afraid to call you whenever necessary, especially if there is a needed repair, and pays the rent on time.

Q: What do you see as some of the biggest opportunities for new property managers?

A: If you treat people well, they will treat you well, hopefully. Tell your owners that if they want to have good tenants, they must offer a good product. Make sure your properties are safe, habitable, and that people will enjoy them.

Q: Anything else you want to add?

A: Try to work for somebody at first; don't branch out on your own unless you have a true entrepreneurial spirit, and you don't mind working 23 hours a day. Join the industry associations; they will teach you the practical knowledge that real estate courses do not.

MATT MIDDEL

"In times of rapid change, experience could be your worst enemy."

-J. Paul Getty

16

"Hire people much smarter than yourself."
Beverly Perina, Armadillo Property Management

◆

BACKGROUND

Beverly Perina lives in Fort Collins, Colorado and is the owner/ broker of Armadillo Property Management, Inc. The company was started over 30 years ago and currently has six employees. Bev manages over 450 residential properties consisting of houses, apartments, condos, town homes, and duplexes. Twenty-three percent of her residents are college students. Her passion is teaching property management to existing and new property investors.

INTERVIEW

Q: How did you get into property management?

A: I got interested in the early 1980s because my father was a real estate agent here in town and had rental properties. No one in their right mind would have attempted to start a property management company at that time, but I was newly married, had a baby on the way, and it seemed the logical course to take care of my father's properties. I started purchasing some of my own investments and voilà, Armadillo Property Management was born.

Q: Did you have a mentor when you got started?

A: Yes, another property manager in Fort Collins and I started our businesses at about the same time, so we grew our companies together and helped each other learn the ropes. Charlie Koons, owner of Mountain-n-Plains, Inc., was also very helpful. She had been in business for about 3 or 4 years, and I knew I could ask her for advice.

Q: Any educational classes that you have found particularly valuable?

A: I'm proud of being very much self-taught. When I first started out, I took several real estate classes at our local university. I read every book available at the time and I still have an extensive property management library. One of the best classes I have ever taken was a continuing education class offered by the Colorado Real Estate Division. Currently I am a board member of the National Association of Residential Property Managers (NARPM) and the Northern Colorado Rental Housing Association (NoCoRHA), a chapter of the National Apartment Association (NAA). Both offer courses locally and nationally for property managers.

Q: How do you keep up with all the new laws that affect property management?

A: The professional organizations like NoCoRHA and NARPM do an outstanding job of keeping members up-to-date on legislative issues in our town and our state.

Q: Are there any specific books, websites, or other educational resources that you would recommend?

A: The very first book I read on property management was *Landlording* by Leigh Robinson. I really love that book and refer to it often. Currently I am reading *The Accidental Landlord* by Danielle Babb, which is an awesome guide to property management. I subscribe to *Mr. Landlord magazine*, *Units* magazine from NAA and the *Resource* magazine from NARPM. NARPM offers a CEO listserv specifically for property managers, with one or two questions daily that everyone can answer or comment on. The information shared there is like having the whole community of property managers at my fingertips.

Q: How do you use the Internet to help you with your property management business?

A: The Internet has boosted every aspect of my business. We were the first company in Fort Collins to have our own website, over 15 years ago. I'm a fan of NorthernColoradoRentals.com, a rental property website here in Northern Colorado which we've been using since it started in 2003. We also use Craigslist and Facebook. I have a young staff and keeping up on current technology has really strengthened our marketing; my motto is to always hire people much smarter than me! Our

> **MY MOTTO IS TO ALWAYS HIRE PEOPLE MUCH SMARTER THAN ME!**

new residents typically tell us they heard about us through the web by searching for rental properties in Fort Collins on Craigslist, NorthernColoradoRentals.com, our company's website (www.RentFortCollins.com), or by seeing our red and yellow "For Rent" signs in the yards of our properties.

Q. Do you do any PR for your company?

A: Networking with all of the groups I am involved with is imperative for our success. Teaching property management classes has been very rewarding as well; I offer classes to established property managers who want to take their business to the next level, to private investors and to new start-up companies. My classes incorporate my proven policy and procedures manual with forms included. I also help teach a landlord class through the City of Fort Collins.

Q: What do you attribute your success to?

A: My passion is for my unique property management business; I'm very hands-on, family-oriented, and have great rapport with my investors and residents. Every day is something new. I never get bored. One of our mottos is: "We are fair but firm." An armadillo is hard on the outside but soft on the inside.

BEVERLY PERINA

Q: When things don't go well, from where do you draw your strength and inspiration?

A: I draw strength from the people that I work with. I don't take on new properties unless we talk about it as a team.

Q: Do you have any slogans that you use or the company uses?

A: "Fair but firm." "Large enough to serve you, small enough to care." "Let our family manage your family's investment."

Q: How do you attract and retain the best employees?

A: I work with the Everett Real Estate Center at Colorado State University here in Fort Collins. During the spring semester we hire one or two students for the summer. These interns will often stay on part-time until they finish their degree, and this has been a huge success for me. We also attract new employees through word of mouth, or just by networking with people in the industry.

> ONE OF THE BENEFITS I OFFER OUR EMPLOYEES — I COOK LUNCH EVERY DAY FOR EVERYONE.

Q: What do you do to retain your employees?

A: We pay competitively and offer health insurance, profit-sharing, and a retirement plan. As an added benefit, I cook lunch for the office; my employees may or may not agree this is an added benefit! All of our vendors and maintenance people know about lunch and will come in and eat with us. We are very family-oriented; my daughter works in accounting and my "bonus" son helps with move-out inspections.

Q: What is the most important attribute that you look for in an employee?

A: A team player is something most people look for, but I think most are unaware of how to actually find and keep those key employees. I value everyone's opinions and fresh ideas. I cannot stress enough how important it is to "hire people much smarter than me."

Q: What are some of the biggest mistakes you see new property managers making?

A: They grow too fast and spread themselves too thin. They don't always make an effort to network with the old-timers and join professional organizations such as NARPM and NAA.

Q: What are some of the biggest challenges that you face?

A. There are many challenges: the housing market, local and state regulations, the economy and, always, parents of our college students.

Q: What are you doing to overcome these challenges?

A: You must be flexible! You have to set policies and procedures, but you also need to consistently update them based on the current market trends and new laws. Our lease language is very strong, and we use an 8-page 3-part form. This keeps us ahead of anything that any residents could throw our way. When we had a high vacancy rate, I was the only company in town to start allowing month-to-month leases and it was very successful. We have more applicants now with credit report challenges, so we require co-signers or doubled deposits to ensure responsibility.

> **WHEN WE HAD A LOT OF VACANCIES, I STARTED ALLOWING MONTH-TO-MONTH LEASES. I WAS THE ONLY COMPANY IN TOWN WHICH DID THAT, AND IT WAS VERY SUCCESSFUL.**

Q: Any tips or tricks that you use to avoid repeating the same mistakes?

A: Talking to other property managers helps a lot, and the articles in association magazines are very useful. I like the CEO listserv through NARPM, and I swear by ironclad contracts.

Q: Describe your best client, your best investor.

A: My best investor has 110% confidence in me and trusts me

BEVERLY PERINA

> **My best investor is someone who has 110% confidence in me and who trusts me to do what's best for his investment.**

to do what's best; he doesn't question maintenance decisions or micromanage his investment. Armadillo Property Management is committed to finding the resident a comfortable secure home while providing the highest profitability for the investor.

Q: What have been the most rewarding aspects of your property management business?

A: I've loved meeting so many interesting investors and residents over the 30 years I have been managing property. Some are artists, writers or people who just have some great personalities and stories.

Q: What do you see as some of the biggest opportunities for new property managers?

A: There are thousands of opportunities available. You just need to find your niche and run with it. Study the market, read books, take classes, and talk to other property managers and professionals in your community.

Armadillo Property Management

17

"You have to be patient, willing to change, and you have to listen."

Diana Pittro, RMK Management Company

◆

BACKGROUND

Diana Pittro lives in Chicago, Illinois. She has more than 20 years of experience in the property management industry. She currently manages 22 properties, including garden-type, high-rise, and subsidized units – representing over 9,000 units in Chicago and Minnesota. Diana has received numerous awards, including the Supervisor of the Year award from her local apartment association.

INTERVIEW

Q: How did you get started in property management?

A: I started working for a condo developer in Chicago about 20 years ago, then went into rental management. I am currently vice president of the management division at RMK Management Company.

Q: Did you have a mentor when you first started in property management?

A: Yes, he was a very tough taskmaster who had me in tears on occasion! I worked long hours, seven days a week. But in the end, he was a great teacher and I've used what he taught me many times since then.

Q: Are there any educational classes that you have taken that you have found to be particularly beneficial?

A: Classes are always worth it; I've taken leadership, motivational, and financial budgeting courses. I've also taken what

DIANA PITTRO

you would call the "designation classes" in our industry, which are provided by the Institute of Real Estate Management (IREM) and the National Apartment Association (NAA).

Q: Do you have any books that you would recommend?
A: The NAA Bookstore is a great resource. It's really the easiest place to go, and they have books on everything: leadership, customer service, resident retention and budgeting.

Q: Any other educational resources or websites that you would recommend?
A: GraceHill.com is a very useful website, especially when you're dealing with fair housing issues.

Q: Do you belong to any associations? I know you belong to the apartment association--any others?
A: I belong to the Apartment Building Owners and Managers Association (ABOMA) and serve on their board of directors. I am a member of IREM and a board member of NAA.

Q: How have these organizations helped you?
A: Their lobbyists keep their ears to the ground on legislative issues, which keeps me informed. This also helps managers and associations to get their opinions heard before new laws are put in place. If you're in this industry, you owe it to yourself to belong to one or more of these associations.

Q: How can these organizations provide more benefit or value to its members?
A: A key value is networking, and I can't tell you how valuable that is to me. I can pick up the phone and call anybody in the country with a question about a problem I'm having, or merely ask about what is going on in his market or particular area. If you don't make use of that networking

> **THE NAA BOOKSTORE IS A GREAT RESOURCE. IT REALLY IS THE EASIEST PLACE TO GO, AND THEY HAVE EVERYTHING.**

RMK MANAGEMENT COMPANY

capability, you'll be sitting on an island by yourself.

Q: How has the Internet helped you and do you tap into any of the social media networks?

A: The Internet has forced us to look at marketing and how we operate in a very different way, and consequently we've found that 40-60% of our traffic now comes from an Internet source. It saves time and is convenient; the only frustration I have with it is how quickly things become outdated, but the benefits are clear. We now focus almost exclusively on Internet marketing, dropping newspaper and other print ads, even for hiring. We've also started using social media tools like Facebook, YouTube, MySpace, Flickr and Craigslist. We offer neighborhood blogs, and send e-mails out to residents and prospects twice a month.

> **THE VALUE YOU GET OUT OF THESE ORGANIZATIONS IS DIRECTLY RELATED TO HOW MUCH YOU PUT INTO IT. A KEY VALUE IS NETWORKING.**

Q: What do you attribute your success to?

A: You have to be very flexible and patient by nature. You have to be willing to embrace change in this industry, maybe more than in other industries. You have to listen to others, and be able to change your methods if they're not working for you.

Q: Where do you draw your inspiration from when things don't go as well as you would like?

A: I rely on my families and my great team of regionals, janitors, and my boss. If we can't resolve something together, I turn to my network of friends in the associations I belong to; the support in this industry is wonderful.

Q: Do you have any slogans that you operate by?

A: "Never use the word 'can't'." When you think you "can't" do it, step back and take another look at it. Maybe ask someone

Diana Pittro

else to look at it with you. I have never found anything we can't do.

Q: How do you attract and retain the best employees?
A: We typically fill positions by word-of-mouth. We're very people-oriented and listen closely to our residents and employees. Roughly 23% of our employees have been with us for over 10 years, some as long as 20 years.

> **We are now on Facebook, YouTube, MySpace, Flickr and Craigslist. For the most part, we stopped using the newspaper several years ago.**

Q: What is one of the most important attributes you look for in an employee?
A: I try to promote from within for a key position, but if I can't, I'll interview someone with management experience and, even more importantly, a can-do attitude. I need somebody who's willing to get in there and do whatever needs to be done.

Q: What are some of the biggest mistakes you see new property managers making?
A: They have a tendency to stay in the office rather than getting out, walking their hallways and apartments, and connecting with residents or prospects. A boss once told me, "If you are wearing heels all day, you are not walking your property." And that's true.

Q: What are some of the biggest challenges that you face?
A: The biggest challenge is dealing with the human aspect of our business, the emotional and personal issues that our residents will present to us. You want to be sympathetic, but you have to have limits.

Q: Do you have any tips or tricks on how to avoid repeating the same mistake?

RMK Management Company

A: When I've made a mistake that I regretted, it's because I didn't listen to my own warnings about it. Trust yourself.

Q: Tell me about your best owner.
A: The best owner is someone who is supportive and listens very attentively.

Q: What do you find are the most rewarding aspects of the property management business?
A: If you do your job well, tenants will be happy and stay, which in turn makes the overall performance of your property a lot easier to maintain. Helping people is the most rewarding thing, but you have to be patient and flexible to stay in the business long; this is definitely not a nine-to-five job. Managers who stay beyond the third or fourth year are in it forever, because they love the people aspect of the job.

Q: What do you see as one of the biggest opportunities for new property managers?
A: The biggest opportunity is being able to get a college degree in property management; a few years ago, the only way to take a class was from an industry association. Now people are looking at this as a chosen profession rather than something they "get into by accident". We've become a lot more credible and professional.

> THE BIGGEST THING I SEE IN THIS INDUSTRY IS THAT WE'VE BECOME A LOT MORE CREDIBLE AND PROFESSIONAL. YOU CAN GO TO COLLEGE NOW AND GET A DEGREE IN PROPERTY MANAGEMENT.

DIANA PITTRO

101

"A competitive world offers two possibilities. You can lose. Or, if you want to win, you can change."

-Lester Thurow

18

"I surround myself with amazing people and I'm not afraid to work long hours."
Melissa Prandi, PRANDI Property Management, Inc., CRMC

◆

BACKGROUND

Melissa Prandi, RMP, MPM, lives in San Rafael, California. She specializes in residential property and Home Owners' Association (HOA) management. Melissa is an accomplished author of several books on the industry, and owns two property management companies. The first is PRANDI Property Management, Inc., CRMC (Certified Residential Management Company) in San Rafael. She has 10 employees, managing 500 residential properties.

Her newest company, of which she is a part owner, is PropertyADVANTAGE (San Diego, California). PropertyADVANTAGE has 35 employees. This company manages 22 HOAs (about 3,000 units) and about 1,000 residential units, and continues to grow rapidly.

INTERVIEW

Q: How did you get into property management?

A: I started as the receptionist of a company when I was 19 years old, and I barely even knew how to use a calculator. I advanced to assistant property manager, got my real estate license, and worked for the previous owners for about five years. In 1987 I became owner of the company and changed the name to PRANDI Property Management, Inc.

Q: Did you have a mentor at the time?

A: My father was my first mentor; he taught me that you have to work hard in your job, to start at the bottom and learn every part of the business before working your way up to the top. I followed his advice, and I've also surrounded myself with amazing, hardworking people. Ivan Maxwell, nicknamed Rocky, taught me a tremendous amount about the property management business. I was very blessed to have him as a mentor.

Q: What educational classes have you taken that you have found particularly valuable?

A: Anything and everything! I've been a member of the National Association of Residential Property Management (NARPM) for almost 17 years now, since attending my first national convention. I have taken every designation course ever offered within that association. I've never missed a national convention, and I was a member of the national board for almost nine years.

> **I CO-AUTHORED THE RECENTLY PUBLISHED (2009) BOOK TITLED, *THE IDIOT'S GUIDE TO SUCCESS AS A PROPERTY MANAGER*.**

Q: How do you keep up with all the new laws that affect property management?

A: We always attend the NARPM conferences, because you learn so much about what's going on in the industry. Once a year we go to Sacramento with everyone in the property management industry. We network, we learn about what's new, and we try to make a difference in the legislation.

Q: Tell me about the book that just came out that you co-authored.

A: It is part of the "Idiot's Guide" series, and it's titled *The Idiot's Guide to Success as a Property Manager*. The book talks about the various career paths that you can go through in property management, such as residential, commercial, va-

PRANDI PROPERTY MANAGEMENT, INC., CRMC

cation rentals, and many more.

Q: A few years back you wrote another book. What was that?

A: My first book was truly my pride and joy because it was written for a large audience: *The Unofficial Guide to Managing Rental Property*. I love what I do and it was so much fun to write a book about it. I tried to educate people about how difficult property management is, that there is so much more to it than just collecting rents.

Q: Any other books you would recommend?

A: Each of my employees receives a book called *The Four Agreements: A Practical Guide to Personal Freedom* by Don Miguel Ruiz. It says: "don't assume" and "don't take it personally." It's a fabulous book.

Q: Do you use any of the social networking tools like Facebook, Twitter, or LinkedIn?

A: We have a blog, and use Facebook, LinkedIn, Constant Contact, and Twitter, where we post rental updates. My son is 22 and works in the business, and two of my other employees are under 24. The three of them are in charge of all of the latest social networking tools and they spin circles around me.

> **THE FIRST BOOK THAT I WROTE WAS TITLED THE *UNOFFICIAL GUIDE TO MANAGING RENTAL PROPERTY*.**

Q: Are you still using traditional advertising?

A: I only do a few of the specialty runs, like a special home section. I have a small ad in the local chamber of commerce newspaper, and on the local Internet Yellow Pages. I think you have to be a little creative.

Q: What else do you do for your marketing and PR?

A: It's really important to stay on top of your marketing. We

MELISSA PRANDI

participate in chamber events, board of realtors' events, community events and general networking. We also have name badges, shirts, sweaters, and blank note cards with our logos on them. We still believe that old-fashioned "Thank You" cards are very important, and every single referral that comes through the door gets a handwritten note card.

Q: What do you attribute your success to?

A: I'm not afraid to work long hours; this is not a nine-to-five job. I've gotten to know, and learned from, good managers who were successful. I hire really good employees, empower them and value them. When I teach a class, I learn a lot from my students as well. If you are familiar with Michael Gerber's book, *The E-Myth Revisited*, he talks about working in your business versus working on your business. So part of my success is due to following these principles too.

> **I WASN'T AFRAID TO SIT DOWN AND HAVE COFFEE WITH SOMEBODY THAT I ADMIRED TO FIND OUT WHY THEY WERE SUCCESSFUL.**

Q: When things get a little bleak in the business where do you draw your strength and inspiration?

A: I don't take things personally. If somebody's really upset, I take it to heart; I'll take responsibility and apologize. We'll improve our training or customer service when need be. It's not easy; the best way for me to deal with stress is through music. I love music.

Q: Are there any particular slogans that you use or your company uses?

A: "The most trusted name in property management." "Property management is our only business: we do not buy and sell real estate."

Q: How do you attract and retain the best employees?

A: My company is like family; we have group discussions, have

PRANDI PROPERTY MANAGEMENT, INC., CRMC

lunch together often, and support each other. I pay well, offer excellent health benefits, and I value my employees' personal time with their families. I am also lucky to work with my 22-year-old son Matt, who was practically "born in the business." He has his real estate license and does leasing, marketing and property management.

Q: What is the most important attribute you look for in employees?

A: They don't have to have property management skills; they need to be people-oriented, detail-oriented, good problem-solvers, and willing to learn. I want them to love what they do. It's a hard job; it's not for everybody.

Q: What are you doing now in your property management business that you feel maybe you should have done sooner?

A: When you know something is not working, cut the loss, don't keep hanging on. That took me a long time to learn.

Q: What mistakes do you see new property managers making?

A: They think they can easily start a property management company, that it's just collecting rent. You need to start small, build a foundation, and get as much education as you can. It's a really difficult job and you have to take it gradually.

Q: What are some of the biggest challenges that you face?

A: I wish I had more hours in a day and could keep up with technology. I am so used to doing everything, helping everybody, serving on four boards, and I love it. But, there is only so much time in a day. I think that's my biggest challenge, you know – Type A personality.

Q: How would you describe your best owner and your best tenant?

A: The best owner is one who tried to manage his own property and failed miserably, because now he understands how difficult it is; he's experienced being "stood up" at a showing,

MELISSA PRANDI

or having to evict a tenant. Good clients are usually referrals from colleagues or friends. The best tenants show up on
time for appointments, pay rent in a timely way, and have paperwork all in place. I value anyone who takes the time to present himself professionally, whether it's an owner or a tenant.

> **THE MOST REWARDING ASPECT OF MY PROPERTY MANAGEMENT CAREER HAS BEEN THE FRIENDSHIPS I'VE MADE ALONG THE WAY.**

Q: What's been the most rewarding aspect of your property management career?

A: The most rewarding thing has been giving back by writing books and teaching thousands of people at workshops. I really value the friendships I've made along the way.

Q: What do you see as some of the biggest opportunities for new property managers?

A: Property management is now a recognized professional industry. That's an opportunity for many to actually be formally educated if they choose property management as their career.

PRANDI PROPERTY MANAGEMENT, INC., CRMC

19

"New employees should be eager, motivated, and inventive."

Jennifer S. Ruelens, ARM

◆

BACKGROUND

Jennifer Ruelens lives in Mechanicsburg, Pennsylvania. She began her career over five years ago as an assistant property manager for Property Management, Inc. After only 14 months, she was promoted to a full-fledged manager responsible for a 300-unit, garden style apartment complex. She most recently worked for Triple Crown Corporation where she managed four sites, totaling 469 luxury town homes and one apartment complex, with a staff of 16 people. Jennifer is now pursuing an MBA degree full-time.

INTERVIEW

Q: How did you get into property management?

A: I kind of fell into it. I needed a job and found a leasing agent position, which gave me the opportunity to do some selling and learn a new type of business. I was eager to take that on.

Q: Did you have a mentor at the time?

A: After I started my first management job, one of my supervisors, Sandy Hauenstein, CPM, became a mentor to me. I have lunch with her regularly and I really value having her in my career; she lets me bounce ideas off her and gives me guidance.

Q: What education classes have you taken that you have found particularly valuable to you?

A: In Pennsylvania, you need to have a real estate license, which is 80 hours of licensing courses. That was quite valuable, but most of the initial training was learning on the job, especially when it comes to property management. I got my Accredited Residential Manager (ARM) certification, which thoroughly covered what an on-site manager needs to know. I've taken Certified Property Manager (CPM) courses, and attended leadership and management seminars. What has been really valuable is what I have taken through the Institute for Real Estate Management (IREM). IREM offers a nice baseline curriculum but, more importantly, it puts you into a room with a really diverse set of people. You have the opportunity to meet people from all over the country, with experience in managing all different types of properties.

> **ANY COURSE FROM THE INSTITUTE FOR REAL ESTATE MANAGEMENT (IREM) IS WORTH ITS WEIGHT IN GOLD. ANOTHER GREAT RESOURCE IS GRACEHILL.COM AND IT'S FREE.**

Q: One of the things that seem to be pretty important in property management is keeping up with all the laws. Sometimes they are different from state to state. How do you keep up?

A: Trade publications, IREM and the National Apartment Association (NAA) will keep you updated. We all maintain memberships in those associations and have great relationships with the regional judges, district magistrates, and lawyers we work with. In our area, there are only two lawyers in this industry, both very active in our associations. They host workshops and seminars as well.

Q: Any recommended books, websites, or other educational resources, that you have found particularly useful?

A: Any course from IREM is worth its weight in gold. A terrific free resource is www.GraceHill.com, a website with a ton of articles and online chats with industry experts. They offer transcripts of the chats so you can read them at a later date. They have all kinds of topics, including blank forms, and oth-

JENNIFER S. RUELENS, ARM

er really cool information.

Q: Have you found the Internet to be something that's useful in property management?

A: Yes. In property management, you need to know everything about buildings, construction, landscaping, plants, different business disciplines, etc. So whenever I'm caught not knowing something, I just go to the Internet and learn about it.

Q: As far as social media networks are concerned, have you found any to be useful in the property management area?

A: We used e-mail communication with our residents and that worked just fine. Perhaps in communities, especially where you might have a lot of students, social media tools may be the best way to communicate with them. Personally, I think LinkedIn is awesome. It's the best thing ever, but I never use it in my property management.

Q: What about traditional advertising like newspapers?

A: No. Newspapers are very limited and most demographics don't read the newspaper any more.

Q: What do you attribute your success to?

A: I am a very, very, hard worker. I was raised by an entrepreneurial family, who taught me that that's what you do. You care about the company, you treat it like it's your own, and you work really hard for it. It has come very naturally to me.

Q: Where do you draw your strength or your inspiration from, when things get particularly bleak or you have a particularly bad day?

A: When things get bad, it's tough to get it together; it requires a lot of you. I think the residents have to be your primary motivation; you can get a lot of inspiration and satisfaction from them because you are so involved in their lives. You are providing them a home, and a lot of times, you're providing play activities for their children.

JENNIFER S. RUELENS, ARM

Q: Do you have particular slogans that come to mind when you come up against some challenges?

A: In middle school, my teacher used this quote, "Today is the tomorrow that you worried about yesterday." Now, if I am not looking forward to something that's going to be a challenge, I say to myself, "You know what? I worried about things like this before and have gotten through it just fine. It's really not that bad." That really gives me the confidence to just embrace it, to do it. I love that little quote.

> **NEW EMPLOYEES NEED TO BE VERY EAGER, MOTIVATED, AND INVENTIVE.**

Q: From your perspective, what do you see as the most important attribute or attributes for a new employee?

A: I like to see employees who are very eager, motivated, and inventive. When problems come up, they go to their supervisor with potential solutions. They are proactive, good listeners, and always willing to learn something new.

Q: Is there anything that you are doing now that you wish you had started doing earlier or sooner?

A: Networking and getting more involved with the industry. I was very young and everybody was much older than me. It was an intimidating process; however, it comes a lot more naturally the more secure you become in yourself, and the benefits are just incredible. Networking, creating and maintaining those relationships, and building on them all the time, are necessary for furthering your career.

Q: What do you see as the biggest mistakes that new property managers are making?

A: Don't believe everything you are told. You're constantly depending on others for information you need. People are not malicious, but they taint their information with personal viewpoints and you need to be objective. You have to use these people, but you also need to go see for yourself. I read

JENNIFER S. RUELENS, ARM

an article in a trade magazine in which a 50-year veteran in the business was asked, "Give your best advice to property managers." He said, "Go see. Always go see." When you "go see," you get a more realistic picture.

Q: What are some of the biggest challenges that you face and how do you overcome these challenges?

A: My biggest challenge is not having a lot of experience because I am so young. If I don't know something and the only way to get the experience is to live it, I need to do the next best thing, read about it, talk to people, and take courses.

Q: Describe for me your best residents.

A: My best residents are financially secure, friendly, and reasonable; they understand our relationship and that my job is to provide them with the best possible housing. Their requests don't go through the sky, and they realize that I don't have to do whatever they tell me to do. They are concerned about their communities, take an active role in the community's activities, offer great ideas on problems or improvements, and they let you know in an appropriate manner.

Q: What has been the most rewarding aspect of property management for you?

A: The most rewarding thing has been the diversity of experience I have had, especially now that I'm in an MBA program. I have been privileged to have a job that's allowed me to work in operations, human resources, marketing, negotiating, budgeting – every aspect of it. Having the opportunity to help other people is even more rewarding.

Q: What do you see as the biggest opportunity for new property managers?

A: The new focus on sustainability is very important, a big opportunity with many implications and challenges for our industry. When we retrofit buildings, we now put a larger focus on new green building initiatives. We also start looking

JENNIFER S. RUELENS, ARM

at our return on investment (ROI) in a different way when we include intangibles like "impact on our environment." It will be a real challenge with owners who are used to calculating ROI with only tangible benefits. "New blood" in the business is going to help a lot with this. If you can come into property management with that kind of background, or just that kind of passion, you will make a big difference.

> **THE NEW FOCUS ON SUSTAINABILITY IS VERY IMPORTANT, A BIG OPPORTUNITY WITH MANY IMPLICATIONS AND CHALLENGES FOR OUR INDUSTRY.**

JENNIFER S. RUELENS, ARM

"When you think you know it all, you don't."
Raymond Scarabosio, Jackson Group Property Management

◆

BACKGROUND

Raymond Scarabosio lives in San Francisco, California. Raymond is the owner of Jackson Group Property Management, which has four full-time employees and one part-time employee. The company manages approximately 485 units: 5% commercial properties, 30% single-family dwellings, and 65% apartment buildings with two to 45 units each.

INTERVIEW

Q: How did you get into property management?

A: It's truly a family-owned business, founded by my grandparents and my parents in 1982. I started back then as an assistant property manager, then became a full property manager at the ripe age of 21.

Q: Did you have any mentors at the time?

A: At the time, solely my parents and grandparents.

Q: What kind of educational classes have you taken that you've found particularly valuable?

A: I was self-taught for the majority of my career. Mostly it was trial and error in the beginning, because I was a stubborn person in my mid-twenties and thought I knew everything. I eventually joined the Professional Property Managers Association (PPMA), a local property management group that grew into a very viable organization which now represents about 20,000 units in San Francisco.

Q: How do you keep up with all the various laws in California that affect property management?

A: It's very important to keep up-to-date on the constantly changing legislative issues, especially in San Francisco, where there is rent control. There are plenty of websites to check for weekly updates at the national, state, and local levels; a very good one is www.Arello.com. It also helps that we have friends at the state capitol in Sacramento.

Q: Any recommended books, websites, or other educational resources that you'd recommend?

A: I joined the National Association of Residential Property Managers (NARPM, www.narpm.com). It was great getting information from others who have been in the business for so many years. The Institute of Real Estate Management (IREM) courses are very specific to commercial revenue-driven properties. A fellow property manager and a very good friend of mine, Melissa Prandi, wrote an excellent reference book, *The Unofficial Guide to Managing Rental Property.*

Q: How do you use the Internet in your property management business?

A: The Internet has been a real fascination of mine. I use it to research legislative issues, laws, tips of the trade, how to deal with people, and more. There is so much out there that culling only the information you want is the hardest part. I actually wrote a two-hour class called "The Property Manager's Guide to the Internet." We use Twitter, Facebook, and LinkedIn, and I've done some blogging. We subscribe to the great listserv that NARPM has available for its members. The important lesson I've learned from it all is to be careful about what you say on the Internet, because it can come back and bite you.

Q: Can you talk a little bit more about how you use Facebook, Twitter, and LinkedIn for your business?

A: We post our available units on Facebook and on Twitter, with a link to our website. It works tremendously well here in San Francisco. Doing everything electronically, like applications, work orders and appointments, saves us a lot of time.

Q: Do you do anything with traditional advertising like newspapers?

A: Newspaper ads are expensive and are becoming a lost art; I have the smallest possible ad in the Yellow Pages. My new business is coming from people who find us by searching on Google. We generally show up in the top ten of the search results. When I use a site like Craigslist, I can describe an apartment in detail and post photographs, so that potential tenants have 90% of the information they need before they call or see it in person. I end up with more qualified leads and spend less time with people who say, "Oh, it's not what I thought it was."

Q: What do you attribute your success to?

A: I ask for help when I need it, and make sure I know who my clients are. I always question if I could do more, and I'm not afraid to make a phone call at 7pm to say, "I told you I'd get back to you this evening. I don't have the information yet but I'll get it to you as soon as I can."

Q: When things aren't going so well, where do you draw your strength and inspiration from?

A: My biggest support system is the networking and the friendships I've created with outstanding managers throughout the country, people I've met through the NARPM and the PPMA over the years. It's wonderful to be able to pick up a phone and pick someone's brain about handling issues or problems.

Q: Any slogans that you or your company uses?

A: "It's not where you start, but where you finish" – I use that in meetings. "Work smarter, not harder." "Never stop doing the small things." "When you think you know it all, you don't."

RAYMOND SCARABOSIO

Our company slogan is "Small enough to give personal service, large enough to handle your property."

Q: How do you attract and retain the best employees?

A: If you don't love property management you will not succeed in property management. It's customer service to the 10th level, so I look for people with a passion for this particular line of work. Referrals are best, but I also work with a local city college to recruit graduates with a specialization in real estate management.

Q: What's the most important attribute that you look for in an employee?

A: They have to see both sides of a situation. While many think the tenant is always wrong, the owner can be too. It's a bilateral contract. Tenants pay the rent, but the owner needs to keep the place habitable.

Q: What are you doing in your property management business that you wish you had done sooner?

A: I would have started planning an exit strategy, created a 401(K) plan earlier, and taken more time off. As important as many of us like to feel we are, we're not that important! And so many of us get into the property management business not knowing if we're building something that we can sell later, or if it can provide us an income stream after we retire.

> **THROUGH NARPM, I HAVE CREATED FRIENDSHIPS WITH OUTSTANDING PROPERTY MANAGERS THROUGHOUT THE UNITED STATES.**

Q: What are the biggest mistakes you see new property managers making?

A: New managers may expand too quickly without planning for that growth, or take everything and anything to build a portfolio without really examining what they're in for. They should interview a potential owner/client as if they were hiring him, to see if they can work together.

Q: What are some of the biggest challenges that you face and how do you overcome them?

A: Training tenants and owners on policies, procedures and rules is a challenge. We have manuals for both, and we sit down and spend a good hour with a new tenant or new owner/client, describing how we do business.

Q: Any tips or tricks that have really helped you in some way to avoid repeating the same mistakes?

A: Don't be afraid to ask for help from others; when we try to do too much, we get into trouble. Don't discount your value, charge people what you are worth. We're human; we're going to make mistakes. Don't be afraid to tell an owner, "I just didn't do it," or "That's beyond our management duties."

> **THE BEST CLIENT I CAN HAVE IS ONE WHO UNDERSTANDS THE INHERENT COSTS OF OWNING REAL ESTATE.**

Q: Describe your best tenant and your best owner.

A: My best tenant understands that if he pays rent on time and plays by the rules, we'll treat him with respect and play by the rules too. My best client understands the inherent costs of owning real estate. He knows that there are good times and bad, and that his assets will need some *TLC* over time to receive the greatest return on his investment.

Q: What's been the most rewarding aspect of your property management business?

A: Turning a mishandled property into a functional one is very rewarding. The other aspect is all the friendships and relationships I've developed over the years with people I respect, especially through NARPM.

RAYMOND SCARABOSIO

Q: What do you see as some of the biggest opportunities for new property managers?

A: This is hard work, and it's not a get-rich-overnight program. You have to take the time to build a business slowly from the ground up, and be in it for the long term. That's when you'll be rewarded.

Jackson Group Property Management

21

"We look for employees who share our core values: integrity, responsiveness, and accountability."

Jessica Scully, Scully Company

◆

BACKGROUND

Jessica Scully lives in Jenkintown, Pennsylvania. She is the vice president of operations for Scully Company, and the 2010 president of the Apartment Association of Greater Philadelphia. Jessica's company has 300 employees and manages about 25 properties consisting of garden style, mid-rise, and high-rise apartments, and a small number of condominium associations and hotels.

INTERVIEW

Q: How did you get into property management?

A: You could say I was born into it; Scully Company has been a family business for over 60 years. I began working summers at the age of 13 and I couldn't get enough of property management. For a while, in college, I thought I wanted to be an anchorwoman instead, and I took another type of job after graduating. But I soon found myself back in the business after taking an open position as a leasing consultant at one of our communities. I worked my way up from there, and I'm now vice president of operations.

Q: Did you have a mentor when you first got into property management?

A: My two mentors have been my father and my uncle.

Q: What are some of the educational classes that you have found to be particularly valuable?

A: I went through the Institute of Real Estate Management (IREM) and got my Certified Property Manager (CPM) designation. Their program is really great; it covers everything from maintenance to finance and it was hard work. It took me about five years to complete.

Q: How do you keep up with all the laws that impact your property management business?

A: The National Apartment Association (NAA), the Apartment Association of Greater Philadelphia, and other organizations offer good ways to get that information. I get e-mails every Friday with updates on new laws and legislative changes, and at least once a year, the NAA sends representatives to speak to our board.

Q: Are there any books, websites, or other educational resources that have been particularly valuable to you?

A: Getting your CPM is key. We try to put all of our managers through the CPM designation program offered by the NAA.

Q: Do you belong to any other industry associations?

A: I belong to IREM and NAA. Another useful designation you can get is Certified Apartment Property Supervisor (CAPS), which is intended more for managers of multiple sites (regional managers).

Q: How does your company use the Internet, and how has it helped your property management business?

A: The way that we advertise as an industry is changing completely because of the Internet; it's a valuable tool for customer service as well. Many times our residents prefer we use social media tools to communicate, like Facebook, Twitter, and LinkedIn. For example, if the elevators aren't working in a high-rise, you can use Twitter to send out a heads-up that the elevators are under repair. In some of our communities, residents use Facebook to get to know who lives in their community or building.

SCULLY COMPANY

Q: Do you still use traditional advertising, like newspapers?

A: Yes. We have an internal debate going on here at Scully Company as to whether the traditional medias are still useful. Some sub-markets still respond well to traditional print ads, like one of our communities in Allentown, Pennsylvania. It's important to know the surrounding area and the demographics of your potential tenants, such as age, before deciding to use only the Internet. Some people would still rather pick up the local newspaper.

> **THE INTERNET CAN ALSO BE USED AS A CUSTOMER SERVICE TOOL USING THE VARIOUS SOCIAL MEDIA TOOLS LIKE FACEBOOK, TWITTER, AND LINKEDIN.**

Q: Do you do any PR to promote your company, like using TV or radio?

A: We've used PR firms and other advertising for a condo conversion, or the release of a new community. It's helpful when you're developing a new project, but I don't think it's necessary for day-to-day marketing.

Q: What do you attribute your success to?

A: I love what I do. Starting as a leasing consultant, and working every position on my way up, was an unbelievable education.

Q: When things don't go particularly well or things seem particularly bleak in the business, where do you draw your strength and inspiration from?

A: When it seems that something can't be done, it really motivates me that much more to do it. When someone says "No" or "It can't be done," it just means you have to be more creative in finding a solution.

Q: Are there any slogans that you or your company uses?

A: We talk a lot about "thinking outside the box," especially

JESSICA SCULLY

if we've hit a wall and the traditional answer isn't making sense any more. As a company we say, "Slow and steady wins the race," and "Draw on Scully pride to better serve our residents."

Q: What do you do to attract and retain the best employees?

A: People are definitely one of our greatest assets and priorities; in our company handbook we outline how people are one of the strategic drivers of our success. We look for employees who care about our company's core values: commitment to our residents, integrity, responsiveness, accountability, teamwork, and old-fashioned values; which are really important and something you can only find in a family business. We encourage our employees and promote professional growth through leadership, recruiting, development, retention, and communication.

> **PROPERTY MANAGERS GET SO OCCUPIED WITH BUDGETS, DELINQUENCIES, REPORTS, AND OCCUPANCY NUMBERS THAT THEY FORGET TO GET OUT OF THEIR OFFICE EVERY SO OFTEN AND WALK THEIR PROPERTIES.**

SCULLY COMPANY

Q: Can you give me some examples of old-fashioned values?

A: The employees make our company run; everybody matters. We constantly visit all our communities and talk to all the employees.

Q: What is the most important attribute that you look for in an employee?

A: We look for employees who share our core values, and recently we introduced predictive indexing to see what type of person fits what kind of job. The profiles of a bookkeeper and a leasing consultant, for example, should be very different; their skill sets are not the same. It's extremely important and something that I wish we had started doing sooner.

Q: What are some of the biggest mistakes you see new property managers making?

A: Property managers can get so wrapped up in the business side of things like budgets, delinquencies, reports, occupancy numbers. This causes them to forget to get out of their office. They should walk their properties, observe their communities, and see what it's like to be in their residents' shoes. Is the property clean and well maintained, does it feel comfortable? They shouldn't forget the basics.

Q: What are some of the biggest challenges that you face?

A: Our industry has changed a lot for a number of reasons: the economy, deflation, technology; you have to adapt to the market and that can be very challenging. We've had to step up our customer service and work harder to retain our residents in this market. There is so much competition to get new residents, as well as to keep current ones.

> **WE ARE COMPETING A LOT MORE, TO GET NEW RESIDENTS AS WELL AS TO KEEP OUR CURRENT RESIDENTS.**

JESSICA SCULLY

Q: Are there any tips or tricks that you have to help you and your company avoid making the same mistakes?

A: A mistake is sometimes the best way for us to learn. We have a list of guiding principles that we run through, like a safety checklist, to make sure we're on the right path for creating value or deciding a new strategy.

Q: Describe your best client.

A: Our best client is somebody who will take advantage of our expertise and allow us to guide him.

Q: What's been the most rewarding aspect of your career with property management?

A: The most rewarding aspect of property management is the people, both our employees and the people we serve. We put roofs over people heads; shelter is one of the most basic of needs. Providing a home for somebody is a great thing to do every day.

Q: What do you see as some of the biggest opportunities for new managers?

A: Education is the biggest opportunity. In addition to the courses and designations offered through IREM or other associations, college degree programs are starting to pop up around the country. Our industry has gotten a lot more complex, and in the future, will become a more popular career. That will require undergraduate degrees as well as graduate degrees.

> THE MOST REWARDING ASPECT OF PROPERTY MANAGEMENT IS THE PEOPLE – BOTH OUR EMPLOYEES AND THE PEOPLE WE SERVE.

SCULLY COMPANY

22

"My best client pays his rent one day late every month and includes his late fee."
Mitch Stephen, Independence Day, Inc.

◆

BACKGROUND

Mitch Stephen lives in New Braunfels, Texas, and has 27 years of experience in property management. He owns and manages residential and commercial properties, including approximately 1,000 mini storage units in 19 locations, 58 mobile homes on rented lots, 45 single-family properties, and two office buildings. A self-taught real estate entrepreneur, Mitch has purchased more than 1,000 properties. In 2007, The San Antonio Real Estate Investors Association dedicated its headquarters in his name. Mitch is the author of *My Life & 1,000 Houses* (2008).

INTERVIEW

Q: How did you get into property management?

A: I owned a condo I couldn't sell, so I decided to rent it out and become a landlord.

Q: Did you have a mentor?

A: Yes, I have been fortunate to have had many mentors. My first mentors were two judges from San Antonio, Texas, who hired me to turn their rental business around.

Q: What educational classes have you taken that have proven to be very valuable to you?

A: Unfortunately, I got most of my early education through trial and error. However, later I attended many seminars by Ron Le Grand, Jimmy Napier, and others.

MITCH STEPHEN

Q: How do you keep up with all the new laws related to property management?

A: I keep up by attending regular meetings at our local real estate investors club, through my network of friends, and through my attorney.

Q: Any recommended books, websites, or other educational resources that you would recommend?

A: I would certainly recommend the book I wrote, *My Life & 1,000 Houses*. I would also recommend Napoleon Hill's *Think & Grow Rich*, Robert Kiyosaki's *Rich Dad Poor Dad*, John Mccormack's *Self Made in America*, and *The Millionaire Next Door* by Thomas J. Stanley & William D. Danko.

Q: Are you now, or were you ever, involved in an Apartment Association, Residential Property Management Association, or other related organization?

A: I have only been associated with the San Antonio Real Estate Investors Association (SAREIA).

Q: How has being a part of SAREIA benefited you?

A: SAREIA put me in touch with new people, ideas, and techniques. It taught me different ways to solve age-old management problems, by paying people to leave your rental property, giving early payment discounts, having tenants pay deductibles on repairs, using more durable materials, and performing monthly HVAC inspections to monitor the condition of the property.

> **MITCH STEPHEN IS THE AUTHOR OF *MY LIFE & 1,000 HOUSES* (PUBLISHED IN 2008).**

Q: How has the Internet helped you?

A: All my properties are online with pictures and details, which is a real timesaver. I put links to my own property website on other advertising sites, such as Craigslist. I also use the Internet for doing online applications, credit checks, and background checks.

Q: Do you find traditional advertising helpful?

A: Traditional classified ads are dying in my town, but whenever I make a strong push to rent a property, I do include them as part of my attack. I'm only looking for one person, so it doesn't matter what advertising source leads a tenant to me. Advertising may be expensive in some cases, but

> **YOU MUST ALWAYS FOLLOW THROUGH WITH THE PAPERWORK. DOCUMENTATION IS KING!**

nothing is more expensive than a vacant house, and nothing good happens to a vacant house.

Q: What about PR, getting in the media (TV, Radio, or print)?

A: Aside from classifieds, I tried radio. It has not been successful for me, but I may not have stayed with it long enough to be sure.

Q: What do you attribute your success to?

A: I credit "the man upstairs," my wife and daughter, and my relentless pursuit of financial freedom.

Q: Where do you draw your strength or inspiration from when things get particularly bleak in your business?

A: In my darkest hours I talk to myself a lot in the mirror. I tell myself that I'm the very best investor in this city, and I'm going to solve the problems at hand. I also make it a point to get to a seminar covering the issues I'm concerned about. I always feel lighter after a weekend of being around positive people who say, "There is a way," and "I can."

Q: Is there a particular slogan that comes to mind to help you overcome challenges?

A: "There are no great men, just great challenges that ordinary men are forced by circumstance to meet."

Q: What are the biggest mistakes you see new property manag-

MITCH STEPHEN

ers make?

A: They listen to tenants' excuses and don't follow through with paperwork. Documentation is king!

Q: What are some of the biggest challenges you face?

A: The challenges are the political environment and the government involvement in real estate: laws, on top of laws.

Q: How have you overcome those challenges?

A: I have increased the size of my contracts, looked for the habitual movers, and kept my liability insurance current.

Q: Any tips or tricks that have really helped you in some way, to avoid repeating the same mistakes?

A: Don't do things out of order; don't hand over the keys before you have your money. Don't give anyone anything; they won't appreciate it. Give everybody one chance to honor their word and if they don't, it's by the book all the way. No excuses.

Q: Describe your best client.

A: My best client was shown the property by someone other than myself. He pays one day late every month and includes the late fee; I never hear from him, because he's happy!

Q: What do you look for in a new tenant?

A: I'm looking for people who want to stay for several years, so I want to know how stable their job and living situations are. I want to know how much money they make. I try to talk to prospective tenants personally, and ask questions about their kids, schools, and employment, for example, just to help them open up and start talking. I can learn a lot in 15 minutes this way.

> **DON'T HAND OVER THE KEYS BEFORE YOU HAVE YOUR MONEY.**

Q: What have been the most rewarding aspects of your prop-

INDEPENDENCE DAY, INC.

erty management business?

A: What makes it all worth it? It's not the money as much as it is the freedom, the passion, the people, the journey.

Q: What do you see as some of the biggest opportunities for new property managers?

A: New managers will quickly learn that the housing industry will always be in demand.

SOME GREAT TIPS FROM MITCH

1. PAY PEOPLE TO LEAVE YOUR RENTAL PROPERTY.
2. GIVE EARLY PAYMENT DISCOUNTS.
3. GET TENANTS TO PAY DEDUCTIBLES ON REPAIRS.
4. STOP USING CARPETS.
5. USE MATERIALS THAT HOLD UP BETTER.

MITCH STEPHEN

"I like to listen. I have learned a great deal from listening carefully. Most people never listen."

-Ernest Hemingway

23

"I look at problems as opportunities, and I love what I do."

Kyle Stephenson, KRS Holdings

◆

BACKGROUND

Kyle Stephenson lives in Richmond, Virginia, where he established KRS Holdings in the late 1990s. His company currently has 19 employees and manages roughly 850 units in small apartment buildings, communities, low-end and high-end properties in the Richmond area.

INTERVIEW

Q: How did you get into property management?

A: I bought a duplex about 20 years ago, then added a few more properties. I had no idea what I was doing, but learned quickly to manage the properties myself because I couldn't find a good manager who really cared about my holdings. I decided I was qualified enough to make the jump into property management as a business.

Q: Did you have a mentor at the time?

A: I didn't have a true mentor, per se. In the late 1980s I was attending the University of Pennsylvania. Donald Trump is an alumnus, so his picture along with his name, was everywhere at that time during the height of his success. I remember thinking to myself, "If he can do it, why can't I?"

Q: Are there any good books that you have read?

A: *The E-Myth* by Michael Gerber focuses on having systems in place for business owners. I believe this is key if you are to be successful in property management.

Q: How do you keep up with all the different laws that can affect property management?

A: We have a great relationship with our attorneys, who keep us informed, and we're required to take credit courses on the subject to keep our brokerage license current.

Q: Are you involved with any of the local associations?

A: I am a member of the National Association of Residential Property Managers (NARPM); as a real estate agent, I belong to the Richmond Apartment Owners' Association.

Q: How have these associations benefited you?

A: The key with these associations is networking. For any business, it's all about relationships; by helping one another get ahead, we all reap the benefits. I believe an attitude of giving to others is essential for my own success.

Q: How has the Internet helped you and how do you use it?

A: The Internet has transformed our business and we're embracing it more all the time. It's an incredibly important way to convey your message and the unique value you offer. We use Craigslist, but it's a shame that this great resource has been so plagued by scammers.

> THE KEY WITH THESE ASSOCIATIONS IS NETWORKING. SINCE FOR ANY BUSINESS, IT'S ALL ABOUT RELATIONSHIPS.

Q: What about traditional advertising, do you still do that?

A: We still advertise in newspapers. It is probably the most expensive method for finding tenants, but it works for us.

Q: What do you attribute your success to?

A: Hard work, a lot of trial and error, and experience. And of course, I love what I do!

Q: When things get particularly bleak in the business, where do you draw your strength or inspiration from?

A: It's incredibly valuable to listen to motivational CDs and read books on strategies for being successful. I've begun to view problems as opportunities this way.

Q: Speaking about employees, how many employees do you have and how do you attract and retain the best employees?

A: We have 19 employees. I use a thorough interview process that ensures new hires are a fit with our particular business culture. My management style relies on transparency; I keep everyone informed about the performance of the company, whether it's good or bad news. We trust, value, and rely on our employees as productive members of our team.

> **I LISTEN TO MOTIVATIONAL CDs AND READ BOOKS ON STRATEGIES FOR BEING SUCCESSFUL.**

Q: What is the most important attribute you look for in an employee?

A: I look for problem solvers. As a business owner, it drives me crazy when employees bring me problems, but have no idea how to solve them. My best employees understand this, and bring me solutions along with their report of problems. Or, better yet, they just handle things without having to involve me! Those people are gems.

Q: What are you doing now in your property management business that you should have started doing sooner?

A: We should have had a better marketing program from the start. If it had been in place two years ago, when the economy started to falter, we would have been better prepared.

Q: What are the biggest mistakes you see new property managers make?

A: New property managers don't understand that they are managing someone's assets and that they have to provide owners with "the good, the bad, and the ugly." Often the bad

KYLE STEPHENSON

news is more important than the good news, and they do their clients a disservice by not keeping them fully informed at all times.

Q: What are some of the biggest challenges you face currently?

A: Sometimes the dynamics of the market result in a greater supply of rentals than there is demand. That's when you need to be even more involved than usual; you must be more attentive, communicate with owners and tenants, and consider some exceptions to the rules. This might mean being more lenient on applications, or upgrading a place a little more than you ordinarily would.

> MY BEST TENANT RESPECTS THE PROPERTY, AND PAYS ON A TIMELY BASIS. THOSE ARE THE TENANTS YOU WOULD DO ANYTHING TO KEEP FOREVER.

Q: Are there any tips or tricks you have that have helped you avoid repeating the same mistake?

A: I would say, "document, document, document!" We keep extensive notes and have a reporting system in place that helps us analyze problems and take steps to correct them. For example, when we turn over apartments each summer, we look at, and document everything from a vendor's performance to tenant behavior. By the following year, we are not making the same mistakes.

Q: Describe your best client and your best tenant.

A: My best client treats his asset as a business, not as something personal, which is really in alignment with our values. It's very easy to work with that type of client. My best tenants respect the property, treat it like their own, and they pay their rent on a timely basis. They're the tenants you'd do anything to keep forever.

Q: What's the most rewarding aspect of your property management business?

KRS HOLDINGS

A: We manage quite a bit of affordable (entry-level) housing, and our involvement in these communities has made a positive difference in peoples' lives. We've actually turned neighborhoods around. We've made them safe places where people feel comfortable and can allow their children to go out and play. There is no question that this is what brings me the most fulfillment. It's just wonderful, very gratifying!

Q: What do you see as some of the biggest opportunities for new property managers?

A: A lot of people struggle with their properties due to job transfers, a move, or when the market will just not allow them to sell. Property managers will get more calls than they know what to do with if they tap into this market segment. It's going to be tough, with owners not having a lot of money for repairs, for instance. But now is a great time for new managers to gain a tremendous amount of valuable experience, and start generating revenue.

> **WE MANAGE QUITE A BIT OF AFFORDABLE HOUSING (ENTRY-LEVEL HOUSING). AS A RESULT OF OUR INVOLVEMENT, WE HAVE ACTUALLY TURNED AROUND NEIGHBORHOODS. THERE IS NO QUESTION THAT THIS IS WHAT BRINGS ME THE MOST FULFILLMENT. IT'S JUST WONDERFUL, VERY GRATIFYING!**

KYLE STEPHENSON

"It is the province of knowledge to speak and it is the privilege of wisdom to listen."

-Oliver Wendell Holmes

24

"We're in real estate, where you can never know enough people and never have enough capital."
Tom Stokes, EpiCity Real Estate Services

◆

BACKGROUND

Tom Stokes is the president of EpiCity Real Estate Services in Atlanta, Georgia. The firm was created by his paternal grandparents in 1935, and today it employs eight people. Tom has been involved in the property management industry for over 22 years. He currently manages multi-family, industrial, office, medical office, institutional, and retail properties.

INTERVIEW

Q: How did you get into property management?

A: My grandparents started our business. After I got out of college I worked in secondary education, but it wasn't a good fit for me. I got an MBA at Florida State University and ended up getting recruited to the family business by my dad and my aunt. I worked directly for my aunt.

Q: When you got started, did you have a mentor?

A: There was a very smart fellow in our company who held the industry's highest designation, the Certified Property Manager (CPM). He definitely had good ideas and led me in the right direction. The most powerful mentor figure in my business life is John Stevenson, whom I met while doing my undergraduate work at Emory. He has given me professional advice throughout the years.

Q: Are there any educational classes that you've taken that have proven to be particularly valuable to you?

A: I got most of my formal education through the profession-al associations I joined. The Institute for Real Estate Management (IREM) courses are very rigorous precursors to the Certified Property Manager (CPM) designation, very struc-tured, thoughtful, detailed and helpful. The Certified Commercial Investment Member (CCIM) designation courses are equally as demanding and instructive.

> **I READ VARIOUS PUBLICATIONS, INCLUDING *UNITS*, PUBLISHED BY THE NATIONAL APARTMENT ASSOCIATION (NAA), AND *THE JOURNAL OF PROPERTY MANAGEMENT*, PUBLISHED BY IREM.**

Q: How do you keep up with all the different laws that relate to real estate and property management?

A: It seems almost impossible these days to keep up, but I depend on our professional organizations. The national, state, and local apartment associations are very proactive, strong advocates, and keep us very well informed about changes in the law.

Q: Are there any books, websites, or other educational resources that you would recommend?

A: Ed Kelley's *The Apartment Management Bible*, published through IREM, is a book that I keep on my desk. I also read various publications including *Units*, published by the National Apartment Association (NAA), and *The Journal of Property Management*, published by IREM.

Q: What other organizations do you belong to?

A: In the home leasing and management area, NARPM has been an extremely powerful force in our company. I have served as chapter president and on the national board for several years. NARPM to this day is critical to our success.

Q: How has the Internet helped you and how do you use it? Do you use any of the social networking tools?

A: I couldn't operate without the Internet. Over 90% of our communication is through e-mail. We use the Internet to find people, to research projects, and to order materials for jobs. We also use our listing databases all day, every day. We use CoStar on the commercial side, Rental Home Pro on the single-family homes side, and the new NARPM rental database. Facebook has been useful. It's just incredible how fast information moves and how the Internet keeps everybody connected.

Q: Do you use any traditional advertising at all?

A: We used to run a half-page ad in the Atlanta Yellow Pages to the tune of $2,000 per month. Today we have a simple small ad in bold, under real estate management, that costs $100 per month. It generates a few calls so we maintain a minimal presence there. If somebody asks, we can say, "Yes, we're in the Yellow Pages".

Q: How about advertising in newspapers?

A: We don't advertise in the major Atlanta paper. However, there's a specialty social newspaper called *Creative Loafing* that we advertise certain rentals in, because it reaches the demographic of folks who will rent those properties.

Q: Do you do anything in terms of PR for your company with TV, radio, etc.?

A: In the past we've done a little television advertising, focused in the home leasing and management areas. We have an ongoing and active PR effort to get notices, information, newsletters, and articles in newspapers and on websites. Our PR person, Julie Chalpan, does all of that.

Q: What do you attribute your success to?

A: Family values are foremost. We're local, we're straightforward, we're committed, and we're willing to work hard. We have stamina, perseverance, and integrity, and we'll apply

TOM STOKES

that until the client achieves his objective.

Q: Where do you draw your strength and inspiration from when things don't go particularly well?

A: Everything we have in my family and our company is a blessing. It all flows from there.

Q: Do you have any particular slogans that you use personally or that your company uses?

A: "Yesterday's service with tomorrow's technology." "Git-'er-done." "We're in real estate, where you can never know enough people and never have enough capital." "We provide clean, neat, functional housing."

Q: How do you attract and retain the best employees?

A: That is one of our biggest challenges. We want to hire very capable, talented, and motivated employees who want to please, and who exceed the expectations of our customers and clients. We have eight employees and the rest of the work is done by six or seven key subcontractors. We have a very senior core group of people; everybody is treated like a partner and paid off the bottom line, so we're all equally motivated.

> WE SEEK EMPLOYEES WHO WANT TO PLEASE AND EXCEED THE EXPECTATIONS OF OUR CUSTOMERS AND CLIENTS.

Q: What do you find is the most important attribute in your employees?

A: We look for a person who has a desire to satisfy the needs of the customer and client.

Q: What are some of the biggest mistakes you see new property managers making?

A: The biggest mistake that new property managers make is not defining their submarket and geography well, and sticking to it. A good rule of thumb is to locate your business so that all of your portfolio can be seen when you go to the bank and post office, and you can still be back in an hour. Time is money. They should ask themselves, "How many submarkets can you really know that well?"

Q: What are some of the biggest challenges you face?

A: The current economic environment is affecting our clients' and customers' ability to pay us, to refinance debt, and to afford the improvements they need to make on their properties.

Q: What are some of the most rewarding aspects of your property management business?

A: Pleasing people – it's not a sexy business, but it's satisfying. We provide people a home. When we do it well, they are very appreciative and it makes a difference in their lives. It gives families a place to raise their children and to enjoy life.

Q: What do you see as the best opportunities for new property managers?

A: The fact that we're going through a lot of changes in the industry creates plenty of opportunities for new property managers. If you're new to the business, you can get people's attention by offering them unique options, new and different ideas, and choices as far as selling, renting, or renovating their property.

> **THE BIGGEST MISTAKE THAT NEW PROPERTY MANAGERS MAKE IS NOT DEFINING THEIR SUBMARKET AND GEOGRAPHY WELL ENOUGH, AND BEING ABLE TO STICK TO IT.**

TOM STOKES

"In the midst of difficulty lies opportunity."
                                                    -Albert Einstein

25

*"I've got more referrals than I can handle because of
the way I take care of my tenants."*
Mark Walters, MW Properties of NC

◆

BACKGROUND
Mark Walters lives in Charlotte, North Carolina, and has been in
the property management business for five years. He is the CEO
and president of MW Properties of NC. His company has seven
employees and manages over 350 residential units comprised
of apartment buildings, duplexes, and single-family properties.

INTERVIEW
Q: How did you get into property management?

A: I was buying investment real estate; then I hired and fired
six different property management companies over a period
of six months because I had real issues with each of them.
Some of them wouldn't even return calls from potential clients. I decided to open my own property management company, and began hearing from other investors who'd experienced the same problems I had. They asked me to become
their manager, and now I'm getting five to 10 new properties
a week. We've grown 300% in the last 18 months! We are
the fastest growing property management company in Charlotte, and the third or fourth largest.

Q: Did you have a mentor when you got started in property
management?

A: I went to Jeffrey Taylor's seminar in Virginia Beach and was
extremely impressed with the way he ran his business. His
philosophy is based on taking care of the needs of both the
tenant and the landlord.

Q: What other education classes have you taken?

A: I've spent over $100,000 on educational courses over the last five years, including property management and real estate courses.

Q: Any books, websites, or other educational resources that you would highly recommend?

A: I'm a platinum member of Lou Brown's organization in Atlanta. His property management seminar is really good; I recommend his seminars, software, and other products and services to anybody who is trying to get into property management.

Q: What industry associations do you belong to?

A: I belong to the North Carolina Apartment Association here in Charlotte, as well as some of the local investment property management associations. Belonging to organizations like these is very valuable because you learn from the experiences of others.

Q: How do you advertise to find new tenants and new property owners?

A: I don't advertise; I'm a referral-based company. I've got more referrals than I can handle because of the way I take care of my tenants – people love how I treat them.

Q: What do you attribute your success to?

A: The number one thing we do that makes us successful is that we answer all of our phone calls. Your call will be answered, or returned within five minutes. I'm an investor myself, I base my company on what works for both investors and renters, and I treat everyone the same way. I don't care if a tenant lives in a $300 a month rental house or in a $3,000 a month rental house; I treat those tenants equally and

> **PARTICIPATING IN THESE ASSOCIATIONS IS VERY VALUABLE BECAUSE YOU GET TO LEARN FROM THE EXPERIENCES OF OTHERS.**

MW Properties of NC

maintain the properties equally. I look for tenants who really care and will leave a property in good condition, resulting in less turnover and fewer renovations or repairs. It's a lot less work and expense to keep a happy tenant, than to find a new one.

Q: What do you tell your owner when he asks, "Do we really have to change out the carpeting? I'm trying to keep a positive cash flow on this property and rents are down a bit right now".

A: I return the property so he can manage it himself, because I'm not the property manager for him. I set standards upfront for landlords just like I do with tenants. I explain to them that I give a tenant a good property and expect it to be given back in good condition; I look over the property and tell the owner what's needed and what I expect. The owner complies because he knows I'm going to get the property rented. My reputation speaks for itself.

> **THE NUMBER ONE THING WE DO THAT MAKES US SUCCESSFUL IS THAT WE ANSWER ALL OF OUR PHONE CALLS.**

MARK WALTERS

Q: How much more does it cost to get a new tenant versus keeping a current one happy?

A: By the time I renovate the property and get it to my standards, and find a new tenant, it can be anywhere from $2,000 to $3,000.

Q: When things don't go the way you'd like them to go, where do you draw your strength and inspiration from?

A: I'm a very motivated person and I honestly love what I do; I love my tenants and my landlords. I use Buildium's web-based property management software. It's set up to let me be paperless: renovations, work orders, accounts that are accessible by landlords and tenants – it's made my life easier because that information is updated online every day for clients to see. I take two vacations a year because this is a stressful job. When I start to feel overwhelmed, I'll go home for the rest of the day and regroup. But I try not to let things stress me out, because I have a system that works for me.

Q: What are you doing now in your property management business that you wish you had started sooner?

A: I wish I'd used the Buildium system at the beginning; Quickbooks was a nightmare for me! The biggest problem you can have with a landlord, is to screw up his money. With Buildium, everything is kept up for you as long as you make entries on a daily basis.

> THE BIGGEST MISTAKE THAT NEW PROPERTY MANAGERS MAKE IS THAT THEY DON'T HOLD THE OWNERS ACCOUNTABLE FOR MAINTENANCE AND HAVING A HABITABLE HOUSE TO BEGIN WITH.

Q: What are some of the biggest mistakes you see new property managers making?

A: Their biggest mistake is not holding the owners accountable for maintenance and for having a habitable house to begin with. Once they take the owner on as a client, they should treat him like gold, as I do. New property managers should really listen to their tenants and take care of repairs immediately.

Q: What are some of the biggest challenges that you face and how do you overcome those challenges?

A: The biggest challenge I've faced lately, is making landlords understand that they should treat low-end properties just as they would high-end properties. If you take care of the tenant, the tenant will take care of you.

Q: What have been the most rewarding aspects of your property management business?

A: I love helping people whom others won't help, like people who were homeless or just left prison and have a hard time getting housing. I have a more demanding system for them, but I do help them, and it's been very rewarding for me. I've even been featured in newspaper articles. I own a whole street of properties reserved for senior citizens. It was previously a drug area. It's been full now for two years, not a single turnover.

> **NEW PROPERTY MANAGERS NEED TO DO A BETTER JOB LISTENING TO THEIR TENANTS.**

Q: What do you see as some of the biggest opportunities for new property managers?

A: The opportunities are very strong in the field, if new property managers will just put themselves in the shoes of the landlord and the tenant, and take care of them both. If they fulfill their clients' needs, they will be successful.

MARK WALTERS

"We are continually faced by great opportunities brilliantly disguised as insoluble problems."

-Lee Iacocca

APPENDIX A

"LANDLORD EDUCATION SERIES"
by Ginny Sawyer

Neighborhood Services

The City of Fort Collins' Neighborhood Services Office employs about eight people, and provides a range of education and resources to the community. Half of our office is involved in code enforcement for weeds, trash, rubbish, etc. The other half focuses on education, outreach, and resources for community members. This includes a free mediation program, a grant program (we give grant money to neighbors), and our community liaison, who works for both the city and for Colorado State University (CSU).

Landlord Education Series: How it Began

Years ago, some of the professional rental associations in town would work together to hold training sessions, typically on a Saturday, but were fairly expensive. The classes were good and well-received, but it became more challenging to continue them with resources diminishing everywhere. Since the city had most of those resources internally, we started talking to a few people and pulled together our own "Landlord Education Series" in 2006. It was so successful we ended up with a waiting list, and repeated it two months later. We now offer the series twice a year, and expect 30 to 40 landlords to attend each session. With the potential number of student rentals here, and all the city code changes including our occupancy ordinance, this educational outreach is so important.

Landlord Education Series: Student Feedback

The feedback from the class attendees about the Landlord Education Series has been very good. People who have taken the class have come back later with further questions, or to provide feedback and tell me how helpful the class presenters were.

Landlord Education Series: Marketing & Advertising

We work really well with our professional organizations in town, including the Northern Colorado Rental Housing Association (NoCoRHA) and the local chapter of the National Association of Residential Property Managers (NARPM). We also work closely with CSU's off-campus life office, where landlords can list all of their properties for free, and do occasional press releases, which often bring in people from out of town. We include information on upcoming classes in every public nuisance letter that goes out, so a landlord who is receiving a citation for his property will also get the chance to attend a series. I have waiting lists because there's definitely demand for the sessions, but I want to limit class size to 30 or 40 people. If the class is much bigger than that, it gets difficult for people to ask questions and have dialogue with other attendees. I want it to be interactive, not a large lecture hall where people just sit and listen. The interaction is what's really valuable.

Landlord Education Series: Costs

The first time I offered the class I only charged $10. Now we charge $20 for the eight-hour course (two consecutive Friday mornings). This covers the costs of the notebooks, printing, coffee and food; it doesn't have to be a money-maker. The class is approved for real estate continuing education credit, but I haven't raised the price because of that.

Landlord Education Series: The Instructors & Topics Covered

The instructors are almost all local property managers and attorneys, who have been great. There is particularly good point and counterpoint between the attorneys; one typically represents landlords, and the other is the lead attorney from CSU's legal services, whose clients are usually student tenants. The balance they try to achieve in handling leases and other situations is a real benefit to the community as a whole. We also have a lot of city staff participants.

SOME TOPICS COVERED INCLUDE:

Safety • Leases •Evictions
Fair Housing • Public Nuisance Ordinance
Resident Selection • Code Enforcement
Smoke-Free Housing • Rental Housing Inspections
Occupancy Ordinance • Unrecorded Dwelling Units
Minimum Rental Habitability Standards

We've had an open panel discussion at the end of the class, but sometimes it's hard to recruit people for that. We're always trying to identify what was most valuable to the attendees, because so much of the information is very city-specific, people seem hungry for it, and this is really the only place they can get it.

Landlord Education Series: Possibilities for the Future

We are considering making the class longer in the future, perhaps as many as 12 hours over a three-week period. We could spend more time on topics like leases, evictions, and the new warrant of habitability legislation. We are also thinking about recording some of the sessions so people could watch them on-line, if we can figure out how to create a quality video of such interactive classes.

Other new possibilities include specialized breakout sessions on new topics, or updated sessions to offer people refresher courses and more in-depth discussions.

A class for tenants would be a tougher market to hit, but perhaps we could work with the university and even get a one-credit class set up for students.

Landlord Education Series: Advice for Others Considering Creating a Similar Program

Limit the number of attendees in each class so that it's a participatory and interactive event. Tap into your local talent, because those people know the flavor of the community and the particular issues that come up. For us, the issues tend to be about student lease termination or roommate situations. Other communities might have more problems with rental properties going into foreclosure, or with crime. It's a real benefit to have experienced speakers.

Landlord Education Series: Beyond the Class, Other Resources

All of the presenters are a great resource; they are always willing to allow us to share their contact information. The professional organizations provide the experience of their colleagues and educational opportunities as well. Our website at www.fcgov.com/neighborhoodservices gives free access to our *Landlord & Tenant Info and Handbook*, lease forms, links to other topics and to the courts, and also some of the most used forms from the Colorado revised statutes, like the seven day demand letters.

Colorado's Eviction Process
by Paul Farrer, Esq.
Springman, Braden, Wilson & Pontius, P.C.

Paul Farrer is a partner and shareholder at the law firm of Springman, Braden, Wilson & Pontius, P.C. with offices in Denver and Ft. Collins, Colorado. He completed his undergraduate degree at Wabash College and attended the University of Denver College of Law. His practice includes litigation of eviction cases, collection cases, and all forms of representation for community associations. Paul is a former prosecutor in both Weld and Morgan County, is an active member of the AAMD, WCAA, and is a board member of the Northern Colorado Rental Housing Association. He speaks frequently to professional organizations on landlord/tenant issues and real property-related subjects.

Colorado's eviction, or forced entry and detainer legal process, otherwise known as "FED", is designed to provide a simple, efficient way for a landlord to legally reacquire the right of possession of a rental property through the courts. Although there are many contexts involving involuntary terminations of leaseholds, this article is focused on the standard residential eviction that does not involve an active military member and/or his or her dependents. It is intended to provide an overview of this process, in the event that the assistance of the court is necessary to resolve the right of possession of a standard residential rental property. The information presented here is not intended to be legal advice. Please consult your attorney for legal advice about a particular situation.

Preparing and Serving a Demand

Typically, a breach of contract by a resident provides the legal grounds for commencing the eviction case. Breaches of the rental contract may be financial, as in nonpayment of rent, or non-financial, such as having a pet when the agreement specifically says "no pets." The eviction process is begun when the landlord, or landlord's agent, prepares and serves a demand. Although there are additional grounds for an eviction action, this article will focus on the five different kinds of demands that most often constitute the grounds for proceeding in a standard residential Colorado eviction case. Matching the correct demand to the situation presented to the landlord is his first decision. If an incorrect or defective demand is served, the entire eviction case is compromised.

The information contained on a demand must also conform to the statutory requirements. Warning letters or other attempts to notify the resident of a problem, generally do not qualify as a demand. The statute describes specific language and information that must be present on a bona fide demand. Unless you are familiar with completing and serving a demand, you may want to consult experienced counsel about the circumstances of the case to make sure the correct form is used, and it is filled out properly.

1. Demand for Payment

The most frequently encountered demand, is the demand for payment, which sets the stage for proceeding with an eviction action for nonpayment of rent. Other sums due and owed at the time of service of the demand for payment are also typically included. All residents who have signed the lease should be listed on the demand, and the address of the rental should be accurate and detailed. Whoever prepares the demand, signs and makes a copy; the demand is then ready for service. A landlord or his agent may serve the demand. The statute requires a diligent effort at personal service, but also provides for posting in a conspicuous place on the property if personal service cannot be obtained. Usually, service by posting is accomplished by taping the document to the front door. A demand for payment is a "curable" demand. This simply means that the resident can "cure" the problem by paying the amount due within the cure period.

The default cure period is within three days of service, not counting the day of service or posting. Cure is made by paying the amount due, or by relinquishing possession of the premises. The landlord must accept payment in full if tendered by the resident during the cure period. Landlord does not have to accept partial payment at any time, and does not have to accept payment after the cure period has expired. If any money is accepted, the general rule is that the original posted demand is complete, and the landlord must begin the process anew to collect the balance. It is important to review your rental agreement prior to service. Make sure that it does not specify notice periods extending beyond the three days, or perhaps require mailing the demand in addition to service.

2. Demand for Compliance

The demand for compliance is employed when non-financial breaches are the problem. Rental agreements lay out terms that, if violated, result in a breach giving grounds for serving the demand for compliance. Common situations are noise disturbances that bother other residents, unauthorized occupants, unauthorized pets, or failure to maintain the premises in a clean and sanitary condition. As with the demand for payment, these are also "curable" situations. The resident can cure the defect by coming into compliance with the demand or relinquishing possession within the cure period, which is also typically three days of service. Assuming the defect is cured satisfactorily, the resident can continue to occupy the premises.

It is very important to be specific when describing the compliance issue on the demand. Judges want to be sure the residents had enough information to know what they must do to cure the defect. Eviction cases can be dismissed by the court if the judge feels that the demand was not specific enough in this regard. If the defect is not corrected within the cure period, the landlord can proceed with the eviction action. Compliance cases can be difficult to prove in court if the case becomes disputed. It is important to thoroughly document the details of the situation by including photos, police reports, names of witnesses and police officers if appropriate, and detailed chronologies. Many landlords are hesitant to post these types of demands, because they think it creates a hostile or adversarial relationship with their resident. However, the landlord could inadvertently alter, or be unable to enforce the terms of the rental agreement, if a compliance problem is not addressed and rent is still collected.

3. Notice to Quit for a Repeated Violation

What do you do if your resident complies with your demand, but does the same thing again at a later point in time? The statute provides for this contingency with a companion notice called a "Notice to Quit for a Repeated Violation." Now you are telling your residents they must move because there is no more "cure." For example, there is a "no pets" provision in your lease. You see that your residents have a dog, and they admit it's their dog. You post a demand for compliance that allows the resident to cure the problem by removing the dog, and they do so within the cure period. A month later, you see a cat sitting in the window. Your resident has violated the same provision of the lease for which you had already posted a demand for compliance, but you no longer want to allow for a "cure." You can post the Notice to Quit for a Repeated Violation. Your resident now needs to move or you can proceed with the eviction case.

4. Notice to Quit for a Substantial Violation

Occasionally, really bad conduct happens on or near a rental property, in which your residents or their guests are involved. The type of conduct and situation may require that the landlord post a special demand, known as a "Notice to Quit for a Substantial Violation." As the title of the document implies, these violations are not "curable." The resident is being told to vacate because the breach is so severe, there is no opportunity for cure. Such situations include violent or drug-related felonies committed on or near the rental premises; conduct that endangers the person or willfully and substantially endangers the landlord's property, or the property of any co-tenant or any person living on or near the premises; or criminal acts violating state or federal law that carry a potential jail sentence of 180 days or more and have been declared a public nuisance by the proper authority.

Due to the fact-specific nature of these situations, it is important that the landlord obtain accurate and specific information to determine if serving a Notice to Quit for a Substantial Violation is justified, and to include the detailed information as grounds when posting the notice. Law enforcement agencies are often involved in these situations. If so, their reports and personnel are invaluable sources of information for the landlord. Since the statute is very specific about what constitutes a substantial violation, it is advisable to consult counsel for assistance in determining whether serving a Notice to Quit for a Substantial Violation is justified.

5. Notice to Quit (or Notice to Vacate)

The last of the five commonly encountered demands in the standard Colorado residential eviction law, does not require a breach of the rental agreement. This is the "Notice to Quit," also known as a "Notice to Vacate." As long as the reason for terminating the tenancy is not discriminatory or retaliatory, a landlord may terminate the tenancy by posting a Notice to Quit. This does not mean that in any given tenancy the landlord can post such a notice one day, and effectively terminate a tenancy the next. The statute provides for a range of notice periods that correspond to the length of the term of the tenancy before the notice to vacate has legal effect. For example, a tenancy for one year or longer requires at least a three-month notice period before it is effective. A tenancy for one month or longer, but less than six months, only requires a 10-day notice served before the end of any given rental period. Again, consultation with counsel may be advisable before serving one of these notices, so the landlord can properly characterize the term of the tenancy and avoid future problems with the case.

The Eviction Action

You have served a proper demand or notice, the cure period has expired, but your residents have not complied with your demand and remain unresponsive to your efforts to obtain their voluntary cooperation. Or maybe it appears your residents have moved, but you don't have the keys back and there are still belongings in the rental. What now? For starters, you are not the only landlord who has been faced with this dilemma so don't blame yourself. The eviction process exists, in part, to resolve this problem and provide you protection against liability so you can retake possession of your rental.

An eviction action is a civil lawsuit in which the plaintiff(s), or landlord, requests relief against the defendant(s), or resident. In this article, we will assume that the relief sought is a possession judgment that returns the legal right of possession to our plaintiff/landlord. The ins and outs of filing a proper suit are beyond the scope of this discussion; for the sake of simplicity we will assume that all of that has happened as it should, and the case is properly in place for the court's consideration. The court papers will establish an initial appearance or return date summoning the defendant into court. The return date is the first opportunity for plaintiff to request the possession judgment from the court. The judgment may be obtained by default if the defendant fails to appear, by mutual agreement of the parties or by ruling of court. If the issue of possession is disputed, defendant can file an Answer on or before the return date. If an Answer is filed, the matter is set for trial. In Colorado, the statute contemplates that this trial is held within five days, so it's important to be prepared to go to trial quickly if a case is filed.

Enforcing a Possession Judgment

Once the possession judgment is obtained, plaintiff now has the legal basis to enforce the judgment. This is accomplished by taking the court order, called a "Writ of Restitution," to the sheriff who will then assist the landlord in executing on the Writ. Contrary to popular belief, the sheriff does not do the heavy lifting and moving of the personal property left behind by the tenant. That's up to the landlord, and the move-out must be accomplished within an hour! The presence of the deputy is simply to keep the peace and provide direction to the landlord at the time of the physical move-out. Procedurally, each sheriff's department has its own rules and fees regarding these matters. Executing on the Writ through the sheriff, provides significant protection against liability for the landlord. Colorado's statute provides immunity from civil or criminal liability for acts or omissions of the landlord, pertaining to the resident's personal property, when following the lawful direction of the deputy at the time of execution on the Writ.

Landlords who fail to involve the sheriff and engage in self-help, even with the benefit of a possession judgment, run the risk of exposure to civil and even criminal liability. Involving the sheriff, even with the extra time and expense entailed, is a no-brainer when your (now former) resident does not cooperate with the process of returning possession to the landlord. A final step at the time of the physical move-out is having the locks changed. There is nothing worse than going through this whole procedure, only to return to clean up the place and find that your tenant has taken up residence again!

Hopefully this brief overview gives you a basic understanding of the nature of an eviction action in Colorado, and additional tools to help you successfully manage your business. Please consult your own counsel for direction about any particular case.

November 6, 2009
Paul Farrer, Esq.

APPENDIX C

SELECTING THE RIGHT PROPERTY MANAGEMENT SOFTWARE
by Nat Kunes, Sr. Product Line Manager, AppFolio

Nat Kunes is senior product line manager at AppFolio and is tasked with ensuring the effective development, communication, and execution of the AppFolio Property Manager product line. Previously, Nat was a product line manager at Citrix Online where he was responsible for managing the product lifecycle, including long-range product strategy and positioning for Citrix Online's market-leading on-demand support solutions. He led the support team during three major product releases, including a new product launch, and developed go-to-market planning for new strategic initiatives. Previously, Kunes was at InfoGenesis where he was instrumental in growing the company's point-of-sale and reservation management services. Nat holds a BS in computer engineering from the University of California, Santa Barbara and an MBA from Arizona State University.

AppFolio was founded by a team of technology leaders with proven backgrounds creating software that businesses love to use. AppFolio creates easy to use, web-based software for multiple vertical markets. The first product, AppFolio Property Manager, is a complete, web-based property management software solution designed to allow property managers to easily market, manage and grow their business.

Property management laws, regulations, and accounting standards are changing rapidly and becoming increasingly more stringent. Investing in the right property management software is now more important than ever. However, choosing and evaluating software can be a challenging process for many property managers.

In this appendix, we will discuss the past, present, and future of property management software – how the industry has evolved and where it is going. We will show you why and when you need property management software, and help you understand how your business can benefit from the right choice. We will also provide guidance on the features that really matter (including a handy checklist to use when evaluating products). And finally, we will provide some suggestions on where to look for the best solution for your company.

Property Management Software Market Overview

Property management software has come a long way over the years. In the early 1980's, property management software was slow and cumbersome, running on early personal computers. Today, the choices are vast and feature-rich, and many providers now offer property management software as a web-based service.

At first, only a handful of companies offered property management software solutions. This quickly changed in the 1990's as dozens of companies were launched to provide software solutions to property managers. Over the last decade we have seen a sharp retraction in products as the larger software providers purchased smaller companies. The landscape has consolidated back to only a handful of providers, resulting in fewer choices for property managers. In addition, many of the remaining software providers have focused their product development to serve the larger property management companies and real estate investment trusts, leaving the smaller and mid-sized property management companies underserved. However, the good news is that in the last couple of years, a few companies have been launched to address this need.

Two Primary Types of Property Management Software

Premise and Web-Based

Property management software can be divided into two main camps: premise-based or web-based. Premise-based software is run on a local computer with a database, and typically the computer is located in the property management office. The property management company purchases and owns the software, and is then responsible for keeping the computer up and running and backed up daily. Usually the premise-based software provider charges an annual maintenance fee, which means they will only be available to fix problems with their software, not the machine running it.

Alternatively, web-based software can be used anywhere in the world with Internet access. It too is fully maintained by the software provider, so there is no need to maintain a server running in the office.

Another distinction in property management software is the option for integrated accounting. Some software solutions have built-in accounting to create a one-stop solution. Property management software providers without this functionality require that you buy an additional accounting program, like Quick-Books, to get the accounting features. This can be expensive, and some property managers find that getting the systems to sync up can be time-consuming.

Depending on the size of the portfolio you manage, different features may be more or less important, and you should consider how your business will use a specific one. Too many features can make the software difficult to use and cumbersome to learn for your staff.

Another point to keep in mind is that the type of portfolio you manage will affect your purchasing decision. A commercial property manager will need a different software solution than a residential or homeowners association property manager.

Why Do Property Managers Need Software?

Now that you have an overview on the property management software market, you may be wondering if it is worth it for you to go through this process of evaluating a software solution.

Property Management Software Business Benefits
- **Move toward a paperless office:** Many property managers are moving away from using paper to save money as well as 'go green.' A paperless office typically involves e-mailing statements instead of using the postal service, online document storage instead of vault services, or online payments instead of depositing paper checks at the bank. A paperless office can drastically reduce operating expenses. You'll avoid the time it takes to search through mountains of papers, the real estate required to store the files, and the costs of paper and ink. If you pay to store paperwork offsite, this is even more valuable as you can realize the savings by discontinuing this service.
- **Manage growth and increase profitability:** Another reason to look for property management software is to effectively manage the growth and profitability of your company. Good software solutions will have detailed reports and charts for income, expenses, delinquencies, etc., which can enable you to run a more efficient business. With this type of data at your fingertips you can identify problems and quickly implement steps to improve performance. It can also help you find new opportunities to improve your cash flow and profitability.
- **Maintain compliance and complete documentation:** Every property manager dreads receiving notice that they are going to be audited, but a good software solution can make this process less scary. Property management software can help you maintain accurate records and documentation, which

will make an audit go much more smoothly.

- **Increase your marketing efforts:** Some property management software solutions include the ability to advertise vacancies on the Internet (your website, Craigslist, etc). Property management software can make this process much more efficient and allow you to reach many more potential renters.

When it comes to timing, many property management companies wonder when to invest in software. It might be time to look for a property management software solution if:

1. You have Excel spreadsheets that are so complicated – no one can figure them out!
2. You are having trouble managing all the details regarding your portfolio.
3. You feel like you are missing opportunities to generate more cash flow because you spend so much time keeping your books straight.

What about property management companies that invested in a software solution years ago? Is it time to switch to a new one?

Many of these products have outlived their expected life and are being pushed beyond their original design and capabilities. If you are in this situation you may experience database crashes, or have trouble getting support from the provider because they no longer support the product. Training new employees on these systems can be extremely time-consuming as well. These antiquated solutions also have not been updated for new tax laws and accounting regulation changes. If your business is growing, these problems can be a real drag on productivity, and should be a strong sign that it is time to evaluate new solutions.

What Should I Look For When I Am Evaluating a Solution?

1. **Choose web or premise-based software:** The first decision

when evaluating property management software solutions is whether to choose web-based or premise-based software.

Here is a comparison of the advantages of each type of software:

Web-Based Software	Premise-Based Software
Lower initial investment	Data is stored locally in your office
Faster, more cost-efficient deployment	Access is not dependent on Internet connection
No software or hardware maintenance	Most costs paid up front
Access data from anywhere	You own the software
Continuous product upgrades	
Training and support included	

2. **Consider the pricing models:** Another important consideration point is the pricing model for the solution. Many providers charge by user. This model tends to discourage use of the software, as property management companies are forced to try to share licenses and limit the number of people using the software at a given time. A new model that is becoming more widely offered is the pay-per-unit model. This pricing method scales with your business and is better suited to encourage the adoption of the software, as you can allow as many people to use it simultaneously as needed.

3. **Understand the total cost of the solution:** An important note when evaluating the price of each solution is the difference between one-time purchases and ongoing subscription services. Knowing the total cost of the solution is critical because the upgrades, add-ons, and extra fees can add up. It's like buying a car; often the base model price is far from the fully-loaded price! When you evaluate the total cost be sure to identify expenses for items such as training, support, add-on modules, and upgrade fees. These can be

as significant as the original product costs, and should not be overlooked.

To help with your evaluation of various products, here is a checklist with important criteria to consider:

Data Migration (when switching to a new solution) – *Can this product take all of my existing data?* *Can I see my data in the new software before I decide to purchase?* *How easy is the data migration process?*	❑
Complete Accounting – *Will this product provide me with full double-entry accounting?* *Is the accounting integrated and included?* *Are the reports flexible enough for my business?*	❑
Paperless Office – *Will this product support the elimination of paper invoices?* *Can I e-mail residents and owners, and maintain records of these interactions?*	❑
Work Orders – *Can I create and manage work orders (one-time and recurring)?* *Can I e-mail vendors for faster completion of maintenance requests?*	❑
Secure Access – *Is this product secure and reliable with my data?* *Can I download reports?*	❑
Easy to Use – *How quickly will my team learn the new product?* *Is it intuitive and easy to navigate?* *Can I find what I need within a few clicks?*	❑
Search – *Can I quickly and easily search for all types of information?*	❑
Electronic Payments – *Can my residents pay their rent online?* *Can I electronically pay owners?*	❑
Vacancy Posting – *Can I quickly post vacancies online?*	❑

Training – *How much training is included with my investment?* *If I hire additional employees, will I have to pay for more training?* *Are FAQs and on-demand trainings offered?*	❐
Support and Upgrades – *What are the additional charges (if any) for ongoing product support?* *How often is the product updated?* *Are client services managers available by phone or e-mail when I need help?* *How is feedback collected from customers for ongoing product development?*	❐
Websites and Portals – *Is a property management website included as an option with purchase?* *Can I easily post vacancies to my website?* *Can I provide an owner portal for easy access to owner statements and reports?*	❐
Pricing – *Is the pricing clear and transparent – do I know exactly what I'm paying for?* *What do the additional features and upgrades cost?*	❐

Finally, take a hard look at cost vs. value. Try to calculate a quick return on investment and figure out how long it will take you to realize the savings that these solutions will offer.

The Future of Property Management Software

Integrated Marketing
Integrated websites, and the ability to post vacancies to sites like Craigslist.org on the Internet, are new emerging features. With an integrated website, all hosting duties and design work are handled by the provider, making things easy for a property management company. Because your data is centrally stored in the property management software, some provid-

ers allow you to add and remove vacancies with a few clicks.

Online Payments – For Owners, From Tenants

Another offering that is becoming more prevalent is integrated payments. With integrated payments you can accept online payments from residents in the form of electronic deposits or credit cards. You can then pay property owners via electronic funds transfer. Payments are received much faster, as you avoid the time required to process paper payments and deposit them at the bank. This can be a great benefit to your owners as they are paid faster and more securely.

Portals (Owners and Residents)

Online portals are also popular as an integrated product. For residents, they provide a one-stop shop to see important announcements about the community or pay rent online. For owners, they provide a place to see all statements and tax documents associated with their properties. Directing people to these portals can save your company considerable time, since you won't have to mail everything or answer as many questions by phone.

Where Do I Find the Right Product For My Business?

Clearly, a good property management software solution can be valuable for your business. But finding the right one for you can be difficult. Some good places to look can be found on the Internet through a Google search or online peer groups, blogs, forums, and LinkedIn discussions. By far the best place to get a recommendation, is from a peer who is already using a good solution. Don't know any other property managers? Your local chapter of a national association for property managers can be a great place to find and talk to peers.

Here is a list of online places to look for ideas and recommendations:

1. Property Management News, www.propertymanager. com
2. Multifamily Insiders, www.multifamilyinsiders.com
3. LinkedIn – Property Management Professionals group, www.linkedin.com/groups?gid=36805
4. National Association of Residential Property Managers, www.narpm.org
5. National Apartment Association, www.naa.org
6. Local apartment associations in your city

The right property management software can take your business to the next level. By spending time evaluating solutions and understanding what the most recent products offer, you can provide a higher level of service to your residents, owners, and investors.

ABOUT THE AUTHOR

Michael Levy worked for Hewlett-Packard (HP) for 25+ years in various jobs including software R&D, information technology, product marketing, quality, and manufacturing positions. When Michael left HP in 2002, he started a consulting business focused on helping real estate professionals use technology to help improve their bottom line results.

In 2003, Michael co-founded NorthernColoradoRentals.com, the largest rental listing website in northern Colorado. A few years later, in 2008, Michael co-founded NoCoAds, a local advertising network that allows northern Colorado businesses to do targeted advertising for a fraction of the cost of traditional advertising. In 2009, Michael began work on his first book, *50 Interviews: Successful Property Managers.*

Michael graduated from the University of California, San Diego (UCSD), with a degree in applied physics and information science. Michael also has a master of business administration (MBA), with an emphasis in computer systems, from the University of California, Los Angeles (UCLA).

Michael was an executive level software R&D lab manager most recently with HP, where he made substantial contributions in the area of new product development. Michael managed up to 100 engineers and their managers, and a $15M annual budget. He has a proven track record of industry leading new product development, from inception to product release. Michael success-

fully managed the development of multiple releases of many of HP's most successful software products.

Michael also has 16 years of international management experience, including four years working in Bristol, England where he managed an IT organization of over 100 engineers and managers responsible for the development and support of all the IT systems for a customer support business unit in EMEA[1]. While in Bristol, Michael led the effort to implement a new software development methodology within the organization using a very effective management of change (MOC) process.

[1]EMEA: Europe, the Middle East and Africa.

ABOUT 50 INTERVIEWS

Imagine a university where not only does each student get a text book custom tailored to a curriculum they personally designed, but where each student literally becomes the author!

The mission of 50 Interviews, Inc. is to provide aspiring, passionate, driven people a framework to achieve their dreams of becoming that which they aspire to be. Learning what it takes to be the best in your field; directly from those who have already succeded. The ideal author is someone who desires to be a recognized expert in their field. You will be part of a community of authors who share your passion and who have learned first-hand how the *50 Interviews* concept works. A form of extreme education, the process will transform you into that which you aspire to become.

50 Interviews is a publisher of books, CDs, videos, and software that serve to inform, educate, and inspire others on a wide range of topics. Timely insight, inspiration, collective wisdom, and best practices derived directly from those who have already succeeded. Authors surround themselves with those they admire, gain clarity of purpose, adopt critical beliefs, and build a network of peers to ensure success in that endeavor. Readers gain knowledge and perspective from those who have already achieved a result they desire.

If you are intersted in learning more, I would love to hear from you! You can contact me via email at: brian@50interviews.com, by phone: 970-215-1078 (Colorado), or through our website:

www.50interviews.com

All my best,
Brian Schwartz
Authorpreneur and creator of *50 Interviews*

OTHER 50 INTERVIEWS TITLES

Additional topics based on the *50 Interviews* model that have already been released or are in development:

Athletes over 50
By Don McGrath

Successful Jobseekers
By Gordon Nuttall

Young Entrepreneurs
By Nick Tart

Artists
By Maryann Swartz

Video Marketers
By Randy Berry

Attraction Marketers
By Rob Christensen

Spiritualists
By Tuula Fai

Parents
By Victoria Edge

Scientists
By David Giltner

Wealth Managers
By Allen Duck

Direct Sales
by Kirsten McCay-Smith

Entrepreneurs
by Brian Schwartz

Professional Speakers
by Laura Lee Carter and Brian Schwartz

Learn more at
www.50interviews.com

www.ingramcontent.com/pod-product-compliance
Lightning Source LLC
Chambersburg PA
CBHW021050210326
41598CB00016B/1154